Available soon:

For more information visit our website

www.oup.com/vsi/

Gregory Claeys

JOHN STUART MILL

A Very Short Introduction

OXFORD
UNIVERSITY PRESS

OXFORD

UNIVERSITY PRESS

Great Clarendon Street, Oxford, OX2 6DP,
United Kingdom

Oxford University Press is a department of the University of Oxford.
It furthers the University's objective of excellence in research, scholarship,
and education by publishing worldwide. Oxford is a registered trade mark of
Oxford University Press in the UK and in certain other countries

Published in the United States of America by Oxford University Press
198 Madison Avenue, New York, NY 10016, United States of America

British Library Cataloguing in Publication Data

Data available

Library of Congress Control Number: 2021944587

ISBN 978-0-19-874999-8

Printed in Great Britain by
Ashford Colour Press Ltd, Gosport, Hampshire

Links to third party websites are provided by Oxford in good faith and
for information only. Oxford disclaims any responsibility for the materials
contained in any third party website referenced in this work.

Contents

Preface

Every age appropriates from the past primarily what flatters its own self-image. What we read today of John Stuart Mill is by and large not what the Victorians read. They believed the spirit of their age was scientific, and so studied the *System of Logic* and the *Principles of Political Economy* first and foremost, and later *On Liberty* and *The Subjection of Women*. Later moderns assume that freedom means personal independence. We imagine that we are free, happy, and egalitarian—or at least aspire to be so. So we find our progenitor primarily in *On Liberty*, then *Utilitarianism* and *The Subjection of Women*, and mostly ignore the *Logic* and the *Principles*.

But 'our' Mill is hardly uncontested either. Rightly regarded as a founding father of modern liberalism, Mill can seem surprisingly illiberal today. He became sceptical about majoritarian democracy and sympathetic towards socialism. He never understood 'liberty' to mean people simply doing what they feel like. His enthusiasm for capitalism was tempered by reservations about its excesses, and he eventually urged ending purely material growth and much social inequality. He even suggested regulating marriage and child-bearing.

The account presented here describes Mill's thought as unified by four key propositions:

(1) that humanity's progress, especially as judged by opinions, depended on truth-telling and clarifying what counts as evidence, with a view to placing the social sciences on as near a basis as the natural sciences as possible, by ascertaining the operations of verifiable laws;

(2) a willingness (from the early 1830s) to treat the present as a transitional age, which challenged the assumed rigidity of the 'laws' of classical political economy, particularly respecting property distribution, and pointed to potentially very different forms of future society;

(3) a commitment to individuality and an ideal of self-culture, both to counter the growing mediocrity of modernity, and as ends in themselves which proved the exercise of free will; and

(4) a consistent desire to explain and justify these ideas on utilitarian grounds.

The combination of these arguments made Mill a strikingly original thinker, and among the most influential of all modern writers.

List of illustrations

Chapter 1
An uneventful life

Beginnings

John Stuart Mill was born in London on 20 May 1806. His father, James Mill, was a stern, ambitious émigré from Scotland to London who had failed as a preacher (see Figure 1). His outlook on life, John recalled, was dour: 'He thought human life a poor thing at best, after the freshness of youth and of unsatisfied curiosity had gone by.' He had 'scarcely any belief' in pleasures, and 'deemed very few of them worth the price which, at least in the present state of society, must be paid for them'. Yet he also had a 'deeply rooted trust in the general progress of the human race', which his son inherited, and then qualified (see Figure 2).

In the capital, James Mill excelled as a journalist, editor, and pamphleteer. After writing the first history of British India (1817), he took up a lucrative post with the East India Company, rising to the rank of Chief Examiner of India Correspondence in 1830, and playing what his patron, the philosopher Jeremy Bentham, described as 'no inconsiderable part in the government of the threescore or fourscore millions' of its people. For the Company was the world's most powerful trading corporation, and effectively ruled a sixth of the earth's population. James Mill met Bentham in 1808, and by early 1809 was addressing him as 'your zealous pupil'. In 1810 Bentham installed his acolyte as a neighbour, and

1. James Mill (1773–1836).

in summer hosted the Mills at his country house. In 1812 he
offered to become John's guardian, and to teach him 'to make all
proper distinctions, such as between the Devil and the
Holy Ghost'.

Bentham was a legal, prison, economic, colonial, and educational
reformer, and the leading utilitarian philosopher of the age.
Utilitarianism sought 'the greatest happiness of the greatest
number'. The phrase originated in Stoic conceptions of 'citizenship
of the world', and was appropriated by Bentham in 1768–9 from
the English scientist and philosopher Joseph Priestley and the
French philosopher Claude Helvétius. Bentham saw in James Mill
a well-connected and adept popularizer of his own often
abstrusely formulated views, and a man with talents in the
classics, political economy, and psychology, as well as practical

2. Jeremy Bentham (1748–1832).

politics. Both became religious sceptics. Terrified as a child by the threat of eternal damnation and of ghosts, and deeply resentful at having been forced at university to subscribe to the Thirty-Nine Articles (the Church of England creed), Bentham attacked religion pseudonymously in *Church-of-Englandism and Its Catechism Examined* (1818), *An Analysis of the Influence of Natural Religion on the Temporal Happiness of Mankind* (1822), and *Not Paul but Jesus* (1823). Unnecessary asceticism and using fear to encourage virtue were condemned, as was religion's insistence on blind obedience to dogma and any advantages attached to believing in an afterlife 'replete with terrors', which fuelled an obsessive 'religious anxiety'. Christianity offered no 'temporal benefit' to mankind, and all religion indeed undermined temporal happiness 'in proportion in the extent to which it is entertained'. As a pillar of the constitution, the Church was also an unswerving opponent of political reform. Religion made practising utilitarianism impossible, and vice versa. These assumptions became vital to John Mill's outlook, and underpinned much of what he came to see as his mission in life.

Young John was educated entirely at home in an experiment in the intense inculcation of utilitarianism framed by Bentham and by his father, with the latter hoping that 'we may perhaps leave him a successor worthy of both of us'. The elder Mill famously thought he could write a book which 'would make the human mind as plain as the road from Charing Cross to St Paul's'. Both saw the young John's mind as a blank slate upon which volumes might be inscribed. Their method was to arrange the sensations to which the boy was exposed in the most scientific manner, while avoiding anything which hindered intellectual development.

A prodigy in the making

There was some effort to make an 'all-round' man of John: a sergeant from a local barracks was enlisted to teach him marching drill and sword exercise. But the boy's talents were primarily

intellectual, and he responded well to the intense regimen imposed on him. He began Greek at three, memorizing words written on cards, moving swiftly from Aesop's *Fables* to Herodotus and Xenophon. Then followed English, arithmetic, and Latin, various sciences, and abundant history. On morning walks he was required to give an account of his reading. At 6½, as its title page proudly announces, he wrote a 1,500-word history of Rome, which if not quite worthy of Gibbon, includes words like 'instigation' and 'banishment'. From 8 to 12 came Latin, algebra, and geometry. For poetry there was Pope's translation of the *Iliad* and a fair range of English writers. Mill was obliged to teach his younger sister Wilhelmina as much as she could digest. At 11 he read the proofs of his father's *History*. By 12 he was as fluent in Latin and Greek as in English. Soon came the new science of political economy.

Religious instruction was minimal. Just as, around 1816, Bentham's hostility to organized religion, which he termed 'Jug' or Juggernaut after the Sanskrit word for a huge rolling cart carrying the image of a god, appreciably strengthened, James Mill became an agnostic, aghast at the proposition that a benevolent God could permit so much evil. He confessed his doubts to his son, though John's sisters attended church. Contact with other boys his own age was strictly proscribed as harmful to his development. One visitor, the Radical tailor Francis Place, called James Mill's methods of instruction 'excessively severe. No fault, however trivial, escapes his notice; none goes without reprehension or punishment of some sort', including delaying dinner because of a mistake in one word. These techniques were damaging. As a child Mill had trouble dressing himself, and his emotional growth was seemingly stunted. The historian George Grote's wife recalled him being 'somewhat repressed' by his father; he rarely spoke in public as a result. His later championing of independence and individuality doubtless reflected this repression. At the age of 15, however, he escaped to spend a year in France with Sir Samuel Bentham, Jeremy's brother. He was soon fluent in the language;

its history and culture remained central to him thereafter. Here too, each day was crammed full of instruction of all kinds, including dancing, fencing, and riding. But Lady Bentham remarked on John's 'gentleness under reproof and thankfulness for correction'. 'Precocious and premature analysis' became 'the inveterate habit' of his mind.

Young John 'grew up in the absence of love and in the presence of fear', for which he later partly blamed his mother. But this may be a deflection from James Mill, whose manner of speaking even Bentham sometimes found 'oppressive and overbearing'. When the upcoming Radical politician John Arthur Roebuck met Mill in the early 1820s, he described him as 'the mere exponent of other men's ideas, those men being his father and Bentham; and...utterly ignorant of what is called society; that of the world, as it worked around him, he knew nothing; and, above all, of woman, he was as a child'. He was 'a knowledge-acquiring machine' rather than 'a human being in whom there were emotions', 'the mere creation of his father's teaching with nothing original'. Francis Place acknowledged his precocity, but thought him likely to become 'morose and selfish'. He had become, indeed, a human incarnation of the many mechanical devices and derivative metaphors defining and defiling the new age.

Mill himself later confessed that the 'description so often given of a Benthamite, as a mere reasoning machine...was during two or three years of my life not altogether untrue of me...zeal for what I thought the good of mankind was my strongest sentiment...But my zeal was as yet little else, at that period of my life, than zeal for speculative opinions. It had not its root in genuine benevolence, or sympathy with mankind.' He ascribed his capacities to his education, not any superior native ability, for in intellectual gifts, he later claimed, 'I am rather below than above par'. (James Mill actually told him that his achievements came from 'having a father who was able to teach me, and willing to give the necessary trouble and time; that it was no matter of praise to me'.) He always

felt 'profoundly dissatisfied' with everything he wrote, a later disciple, the Liberal politician John Morley, recalled, and could proceed only when he applied the same judgment to others. (Students take note: he doubtless found writing painful.) Mill suffered with dignity under his father's intense training. Unlike his younger siblings, he remembered, he had not 'loved him tenderly'. He was instead 'always loyally devoted to him', a loyalty which survived into his own old age. But his was not an altogether unhappy childhood. The Chartist Henry Solly remembered him as 'a great favourite with his family. He was evidently very fond of his mother and sisters, and they of him; and he frequently manifested a sunny brightness and gaiety of heart and behaviour which were singularly fascinating.'

The principles of Mill's education rested on two psychological premises. The first was that the individual character was formed from compounded sensations or stimuli which congealed more or less mechanically as ideas, a view known as associationism, and promoted by Locke, Hume, and David Hartley. The second was that individuals, using a 'felicific calculus', pursued happiness and avoided pain first and foremost, but could be educated to promote the highest moral good: the happiness of all. To Bentham, 'Nature has placed mankind under the governance of two sovereign masters, *pain and pleasure*.' Rejecting moral systems based on concepts like the 'law of nature', 'right reason', 'the moral sense', and 'natural rectitude', he saw utilitarianism as a vastly superior substitute for these and for religion. He famously dismissed the chief doctrine of the revolutionary era, the theory of natural rights, as 'nonsense upon stilts'. 'The feeling rushed upon me', Mill recalled of his first mature engagement with utilitarianism, 'that all previous moralists were superseded, and that here indeed was the commencement of a new era in thought.' This realization 'gave unity to my conceptions of things. I now had opinions; a creed, a doctrine, a philosophy; in one among the best senses of the word, a religion; the inculcation and diffusion of which could be made the principal outward purpose of a life.'

Besides requiring extensive education, a second accusation against Benthamism was that it was a 'pig philosophy', as a leading critic, the historian Thomas Carlyle, rudely termed it, because 'happiness', vulgarly conceived, seemingly consisted primarily in bodily pleasures. James Mill shrugged off such allegations. To him 'the principle of utility...marshals the duties in their proper order, and will not permit mankind to be deluded, as so long they have been, sottishly to prefer the lower to the higher good, and to hug the greater evil, from fear of the less'. Here his son followed steadfastly. The charge that the Utilitarians taught unbridled hedonism could not be allowed to stick. Thus John said of his father that 'temperance, in the large sense intended by the Greek philosophers—stopping short at the point of moderation in all indulgences—was with him, as with them, almost the central point of educational precept'. And so it would be said of him (by Morley) that 'he regarded the two constituents of a satisfied life, much tranquillity and some excitement, as perfectly attainable by many men, and as ultimately attainable by very many more'.

Utilitarian politics

To understand the trajectory of Mill's development we need some sense of how the substantial political implications of utilitarianism were understood by his teachers. Bentham had aspired to be a world reformer, modelling himself on Mentor, the ideal legislator in Fénelon's famous *The Adventures of Telemachus* (1699). Initially a staunch Tory enamoured of enlightened despotism, Bentham warmed to the French Revolution, and became a democrat in 1790. Then, despising Jacobinism, he backpaddled, only to espouse radical democratic principles again publicly in 1809–10. James Mill had worked for the conservative *Anti-Jacobin Review* on first arriving in London. But he had (in Mrs Grote's assessment) 'a scorn and hatred of the ruling classes which amounted to positive fanaticism'. Even Bentham conceded that he 'rather hated the ruling few than loved the suffering many'. Mill now envisioned creating a Radical party bent on modernizing the

constitution and the nation's opinions. This would remain a lifelong goal for John, too, who at age 16 enthused that 'the greatest glory I was capable of conceiving was that of figuring, successful or unsuccessful, as a Girondist in an English Convention'. (Most of these moderate French revolutionaries were guillotined during Robespierre's Jacobin Terror of 1793–4.) John Mill's first 'argumentative essay', written in 1822, was on 'the aristocratic prejudice that the rich were, or were likely to be, superior in moral excellence to the poor'. He never doubted that they were not.

James Mill's politics were defined by his essay on 'Government' (1820), which deduced the best form of polity from supposedly uniform laws of human nature, stated that government should aim 'to increase to the utmost the pleasures, and diminish to the utmost the pains, which men derive from one another', and asserted that 'the greatest possible happiness of society is attained by insuring to every man the greatest possible quantity of the produce of his labour'. He commenced from the Hobbesian premise that all men 'desire to render the person and property of another subservient to his pleasures'. The 'desire to possess unlimited power of inflicting pain upon others' was 'an inseparable part of human nature'. The end of government was defined as protecting property, which was best achieved by representative institutions. Monarchy and aristocracy were dismissed as leaving too much opportunity to plunder the public.

James Mill commended a broad franchise aimed at uniting the interests of governors and the governed, suggesting that all males aged 40 and over should be able to vote. Bentham thought this too old (average life expectancy was only 40 at this point). He even commented in 1824 that young John at the age of 18 'was beyond all doubt fitter' to be a legislator than most MPs. Bentham thought political reform would lead the lower classes to identify their interests with the wealthy. James Mill hoped they would 'be guided by [the] advice and example' of the middle ranks, the

'most wise and virtuous part of the community'. This would be a self-consciously bourgeois revolution—'special pleading for the middle classes' was the Labour politician R. H. S. Crossman's later judgment on the *Essay*.

The Benthamite 'Philosophic Radicals', whose motto for John Mill was 'enmity to the aristocratic principle', thus aimed more at destroying the political power of Britain's 200 or so ruling families than enfranchising the people as such. Extending voting potentially invited large numbers of the illiterate and ill-informed into the political process, with, following the trajectory of the French Revolution, the attendant possibility of disorder, and even the confiscation of the property of the rich. This threat agitated the younger Mill throughout his career. Parliamentary reform was both desirable and inevitable, as a corrupt oligarchy dominated by the aristocracy ruled Britain as what Bentham termed a 'sinister interest'. But how to stem the tide of ignorant legislation which might result? Without the mental and moral improvement of the many, Mill often despaired, the results might prove dismal. For the time being, he wrote in 1839, the Radicals should aim for 'Government *by means of* the middle for the working classes'.

After 1817 radicalism revived, and agitation for electoral reform continued intermittently throughout Mill's life. The plebeian reformers were led first by William Cobbett and Henry Hunt, and then, in the 1830s and 1840s, by the Chartists. In the unreformed Parliament power was largely in the hands of the landed aristocracy and of government 'placemen'. Seats were advertised for sale in newspapers, bribery of electors was common, and many newer industrial towns had no MPs at all. Westminster did not reflect the great shift in economic and social power wrought by the Industrial Revolution, or the ideas of popular sovereignty inherited from the French Revolution. After the first or 'Great' Reform Act of 1832 the number of electors increased by some 60 per cent, and perhaps a hundred or more sympathizers of Benthamism entered the new Parliament. James Mill helped to

organize pressure 'outdoors' prior to the Act, occasionally offering hints of violence if it was not carried.

Utilitarian economics

The Utilitarians zealously supported the new laissez-faire school of political economy, and broadly conceived corrupt and profligate aristocratic government and grossly unequal taxation as key causes of poverty. They believed the interests of the working and middle classes were largely identical, with wages resulting from a competitive bargain 'made in freedom' (in James Mill's terms) according to the law of supply and demand. They had little sympathy for the destitute sixth of the population; Bentham and James Mill commended a harsh regime of poor relief (welfare) to make any employment preferable to public handouts. *Homo œconomicus* was hard-working, diligent, thrifty, ingenious, and anxious to get ahead. Besides Bentham, the influence on the Utilitarians of the political economist David Ricardo, whom James Mill met in 1811, was notable; Bentham later remarked, 'I was the spiritual father of Mill, and Mill the spiritual father of Ricardo.' The latter's *Principles of Political Economy and Taxation* (1817) redefined the subject, hitherto dominated by Adam Smith. It was soon called the 'dismal science', because Ricardo agreed with Thomas Robert Malthus's *Essay on Population* (1798) that workers' wages tended inevitably to subsistence level if population growth was uncontrolled. (James Mill converted to Malthusianism after fathering nine children, or 'brats' as he called them; Francis Place, to neo-Malthusianism, implying the possibility of artificial birth control, after 15.) (See Figure 3.)

The population question was obviously a sensitive issue; Ricardo even objected to James Mill mentioning 'procreation' when discussing it. Malthus was much hated by working-class leaders like Cobbett, and John Mill had an uphill battle persuading them that population control could be seen as a, indeed *the*, progressive doctrine. Mill later wrote that he and his friends, the nucleus of

3. Thomas Robert Malthus (1766–1834).

the new Radical party, took up the cause of birth control 'with ardent zeal in the contrary sense, as indicating the sole means of…securing full employment at high wages to the whole labouring population through a voluntary restriction of the increase of their numbers'. Mill was so imbued with this principle that, in a bout of youthful idealism, after having seen more than one abandoned baby, he was briefly arrested in 1825 for distributing a birth control pamphlet, *What is Love?*, written by

the radical journalist Richard Carlile, and supplied by Francis Place. Sentenced to 14 days in prison, as the son of a gentleman he was released after three or four days. He also contributed several letters on birth control to a radical paper, *The Black Dwarf.* Mill's neo-Malthusianism persisted throughout his life. It was interwoven with his rationalism, and his assumption of a gradual diminution of sexual appetite as the rational faculties expanded. 'I think it probable', he wrote, 'that this particular passion will become with men, as it is already with a large number of women, completely under the control of the reason.' Plato, he thought, had pointed in this direction in his *Laws*, as had William Godwin in the 1790s. We cannot understand him as a thinker without giving this theme a central place in his ideas.

The young Benthamite

Returning from France in 1822, Mill founded a 'Utilitarian Society', later claiming it was 'the first time that any one had taken the title of Utilitarian'. Mocked by the Tory poet Robert Southey as 'Futilitarians', they met at Bentham's house in 'a sectarian spirit'. In 1823 he followed his father to India House for lifelong employment, mostly reading dispatches from and writing to the Indian presidencies. His eventual salary was £1,200 per annum (about £100,000 today). Here he worked six hours daily, from 10 am to 4 pm, commencing with a simple breakfast prepared by the messengers of a boiled egg, bread, butter, and tea, and eating nothing else until six in the evening. The post left plenty of time for other pursuits; his first biographer and friend, Alexander Bain, thought he really spent no more than three hours daily on official business. Most Sundays he took long walks in the countryside, becoming in the process an accomplished botanist. In 1822 he read Bentham's *Analysis of the Influence of Natural Religion*, and a year later vigorously defended its publisher, Richard Carlile, then being prosecuted for printing books hostile to Christianity, and especially Thomas Paine's works. (From this year Carlile also supported female enfranchisement and birth control.) In 1824,

at Bentham's urging, the Radicals founded their own journal, the *Westminster Review*. Edited by James Mill, it focused on combating the dominant *Edinburgh Review* and *Quarterly Review*, which were respectively Whig and Tory in orientation.

The principles of 'the so called Bentham school in philosophy and politics', with its championing of 'an almost unbounded confidence in the efficacy of two things: representative government, and complete freedom of discussion', now became widely known. In 1825, John Mill edited Bentham's *Rationale of Judicial Evidence*, the most complex of the master's works, and one whose chief aim—the clarification of 'proof'—he later developed in his *System of Logic*. Now was born the first of Mill's four key ideas, that progress in all thought rested on well-reasoned arguments and carefully assessed evidence based on observation and experience. This is often termed 'empiricism', and is usually held to commence with Bacon and Locke. Mill preferred to call himself a 'scientist', which invoked greater authority. 'Faith' in *anything* was never acceptable, and merely encouraged unexamined thinking: we will see how the critique of theology—though not necessarily a humanistic religion—underpinned Mill's thought throughout his life. Mill would become the greatest sceptic and humanist of his age, and remained deeply committed to the proposition that the truth will set you free.

The machine breaks down

Meanwhile, however, utilitarianism became a kind of prison for Mill. He was a prodigy, but there was a hefty price to pay. Later derisorily dismissed by Thomas Carlyle as a 'logic-chopping...steam engine', Mill indeed confessed that, like the other Benthamites, he was in this period 'a dry, hard logical machine'. He was dominated by 'zeal for what I thought the good of mankind'. But this resulted, as we saw, not from 'genuine benevolence or sympathy with mankind' or 'any high enthusiasm for ideal nobleness', but instead from speculative opinions.

Tenderness was lacking in his home life. His father, he later wrote, 'resembled almost all Englishmen in being ashamed of the signs of feeling'. But there was a philosophic defence that feelings were unimportant; Mrs Grote thought the elder Mill incapable of 'giving way to feelings of any kind (especially of love)', and regarded 'the cultivation of individual affections and sympathies as destructive of lofty aims, and indubitably hurtful to the mental character'. Young John wrote an essay, later destroyed, 'against all sentiment & feeling'. 'All we thought of', he recalled, 'was to alter people's opinions; to make them believe according to evidence, and know what was their real interest...we expected the regeneration of mankind not from any direct action on those sentiments but from educated intellect enlightening the selfish feelings'. Nonetheless, in 1825 Mill asserted that 'Feeling has to do with our actions, reason with our opinions; it is by our reason that we find out what it is our duty to do; it is our feelings which supply us with motives to act upon it when found.' In 1829 he proclaimed that 'It appears to me utterly hopeless and chimerical to suppose that the regeneration of mankind can ever be wrought by means of working on their opinions.' This was the year, perhaps by coincidence, that the historian T. B. Macaulay, attacking James Mill's *Essay*, asserted that 'It is one of the principal tenets of the Utilitarians, that sentiment and eloquence serve only to impede the pursuit of truth.'

A result of this outlook was that Mill was always serious and very tightly wound. The diarist Charles Greville noted in 1830 that he was 'hesitating and slow, and has the appearance of being always working in his mind propositions or a syllogism'. In 1831, when they first met, Thomas Carlyle described him as 'modest, remarkably gifted with precision of utterance; enthusiastic, yet lucid, calm', but added that 'His incapability of laughing is the most suspicious circumstance about him.' Others recalled that he 'would heave for a few moments with half uttered laughter' at good humour. Slowly, however, in the mid-1820s, he became aware that his personality lacked its 'natural source, poetical

culture; while there was a superabundance of the discipline antagonistic to it, that of mere logic and analysis'. He now saw 'the undervaluing of feeling' as a systematic omission in his father's teachings. An early editor of Mill's letters, Hugh Elliott, thought that, far from being a mere 'logic-chopping machine', Mill was 'a man of such intensity and depth of feeling as is rarely to be met with'. If so, these feelings were often suppressed. But they had to come out at some point.

When they did, in Mill's famous mental 'crisis' of 1826–7, what began as 'a dull state of nerves' degenerated into something more serious. The breakdown began with Mill asking himself the question, 'Suppose that all your objects in life were realized, that all the changes in institutions and opinions which you are looking forward to, could be completely effected at this very instant; would this be a great joy and happiness to you?' On finding that 'an irrepressible self-consciousness distinctly answered "No!"', the 'whole foundation on which my life was constructed fell down'. Why did he not *feel* happy when he knew his great motive in life was pursuing the good of all? Even his love of mankind had 'worn itself out'. This truth did not set him free: it crushed him. Mill now saw the deficiencies of his education, including its inability to specify an antidote. He sank into despair, recovering only on reading the 18th-century French philosopher Marmontel's account of his father's death; concluding that he must support his family, Mill burst into tears. He now realized that he could feel after all, even if 'the habit of analysis has a tendency to wear away the feelings'.

Mill now saw himself as the helpless victim of his education, and incapable of self-motivated action. For months 'the doctrine of what is called Philosophical Necessity weighed like an incubus on my existence. I felt as if I was scientifically proved to be the helpless slave of antecedent circumstances; as if my character and that of all others had been formed for us by agencies beyond our control, and was wholly out of our own power.' Here he referred

primarily to the socialist Robert Owen's key principle, that personality resulted from environmental influences, not innate principles or 'Original Sin'. Then, emerging from the gloom, he found 'I was no longer hopeless. I was not a stock or a stone. I had still, it seemed, some of the material out of which all worth of character and all capacity of happiness are made.' Now he concluded that 'though character is formed by circumstances, our own desires can do much to shape those circumstances and that what is really inspiring and ennobling in the doctrine of freewill, is the conviction that we have real power over the formation of our own character'.

Another insight which followed, Mill thought, was that it was pointless to desire happiness as such: 'this end was only to be attained by not making it the direct aim'. 'Those only are happy', Mill now reflected, 'who have their minds fixed on some object other than their own happiness; on the happiness of others, on the improvement of mankind, even on some art or pursuit, followed not as a means, but as itself an ideal end.' This now became 'the basis of my philosophy of life'. (The late Victorian philosopher Henry Sidgwick later termed the 'paradox of hedonism' the notion that the more we seek happiness the less likely we are to find it.) In addition, Mill recalled, 'I now for the first time gave its proper place among the prime necessities of human well being, to the internal culture of the individual. I ceased to attach almost exclusive importance to the ordering of outward circumstances, and to the training of the human being for knowledge and for action.' Consequently, the 'cultivation of the feelings now became one of the cardinal points in my ethical and philosophical creed'. He later asserted, in relation to Plato, that 'The love of virtue, and every other noble feeling, is not communicated by reasoning, but caught by inspiration or sympathy from those who already have it; and its nurse and foster-mother is Admiration.'

Mill's crisis was thus a crisis for utilitarianism as such, and revealed Bentham's and James Mill's one-sidedness. But it passed:

the incubus was lifted. Wordsworth's poetry, especially respecting nature, in which 'thought coloured by feeling, under the excitement of beauty', was revealed, and music, proved helpful in shaping what Mill increasingly saw as 'many-sidedness'. Now romanticism as well as utilitarianism could claim a disciple in Mill. But he would later suffer ill health frequently, commencing in 1836 with a 'derangement of the brain' which produced a relentless twitching over one eye. Lung and stomach problems followed, and more prolonged ailments in 1848 and 1854.

Chapter 2
Remaking radicalism, 1835–45

Bentham, Coleridge, Tocqueville, Malthus; the *Logic*

Mill's breakdown left him with two issues which would dominate the rest of his life: how can we be said to possess 'free will', and an active, not merely passive, character, if our behaviour is not only shaped but determined by circumstances; and how can the centrality of feelings or emotions in human life be incorporated into an essentially rationalist account of the progress of opinion?

The answer to the first question inspired Mill's account of the self-formation of character, so central to both the *Logic* and *On Liberty*. Mill had been 'made' by his education. But he now insisted that he could make something else, someone else, of himself, indeed that he could not feel 'free' otherwise. But he *had* to feel free: this was the only way of overcoming his depression. Determinism implied fatalism and passivity. Fatalism included Calvinism, which Mill defined as believing in 'no redemption for any one until human nature is killed within him...man needs no capacity, but that of surrendering himself to the will of God'. Such views clearly undermined any possibility of free will, though many sought in the concept of God the safety of *not* feeling responsible for their own fates. The outcome of this chain of reasoning was

Mill's preference, following Bentham and the Epicureans, for active over passive types of character in both individuals and nations. His views of liberty, religion, progress, and civilization were in many respects thereafter deduced from this premise. He now extended the same logic to society as he did to himself, writing in 1842 that 'the mental regeneration of Europe must precede its social regeneration'. But could these generalities apply to all? For clearly we are not all equally 'free'. In the *Principles*, Mill stated that the 'generality of labourers in this and most other countries, have as little choice of occupation or freedom of locomotion, are practically as dependent on fixed rules and on the will of others, as they could be on any system short of actual slavery'. 'Actual slavery' was itself still widespread. And most women were in a state of 'entire domestic subjugation'. How could they have 'free will', if this meant not only a conception of acting differently but also the capacity to do so?

The answer to the second question, respecting feelings, required a thorough revaluation of Benthamism. Bentham famously claimed that as far as generating pleasure was concerned, push-pin, a child's game played with pins, was 'just as good as poetry'. He also thought poetry was merely 'misrepresentation'; James Mill said that prose 'is when all the lines except the last go on to the end. Poetry is when some of them fall short of it.' After his 'crisis', Mill realized that Wordsworth's poetry in particular evoked in him emotions he had hitherto lacked, whose value Benthamism simply neglected. Wordsworth regarded cultivating such feelings as an integral part of 'self-culture', which for Mill now partly defined 'free will'. Understanding how feelings interacted with opinions was equally crucial. This had profound implications for politics, and for humanity's progress, which also became more contingent on feelings. Mill now became much more receptive to other influences, even to conservative critics of Benthamism. A new world opened up to him, and he began boldly to explore it. He was becoming his own person.

Rebellion

This reaction against Benthamism characterized what Mill called the second phase of his intellectual development. It involved encounters with, among others, the poet Samuel Taylor Coleridge and Thomas Carlyle, who are often called 'Romantics'. Carlyle was particularly critical of the Utilitarians, seeing them in 1829 as architects of an 'Age of Machinery' where 'Men are grown mechanical in head and in heart, as well as in hand. They have lost faith in individual endeavour, and in natural force, of any kind. Not for internal perfection, but for external combinations and arrangements, for institutions, constitutions,—for Mechanism of one sort or other, do they hope and struggle.' This left no emphasis on 'the necessity and infinite worth of moral goodness', a message Mill readily welcomed.

A second line of criticism, against utilitarian economics, came from Owen's followers. In the mid-1820s Mill and several friends debated some Owenites in London over three months, with the Utilitarians defending political economy and the socialists their planned communist colonies on the land. As a budding Ricardian, Mill rejected Owenite condemnations of competition and private property, and saw little merit in schemes involving a few thousand living communally and sharing produce while alternating between agricultural and industrial labour. Political economy he regarded as the science of wealth production. Mill upheld its central principle, 'free trade', with an evangelical enthusiasm, and treated economic laws as akin to laws of nature like gravity. He did not yet have that 'fine despair', in the political theorist Harold Laski's term, which later made him 'welcome socialism itself rather than allow the continuance of the new capitalist system'.

In the late 1820s, however, Mill's views altered considerably. He now encountered a group of French socialists, the Saint-Simonians, followers of the utopian Henri, comte de Saint-Simon,

formerly secretary to the marquis de Condorcet, whose promotion of the rights of women as well as a theory of progress anticipated Mill's. Mill took up what would become a lifelong crusade: feminism. His father rejected female enfranchisement, with the *Essay on Government* describing women's interests as represented by their male protectors. In the 1790s Bentham had agreed. But he now lamented the 'universally existing tyranny of the male sex over the female', and condemned James Mill's 'abominable opinion' on the subject. Mill probably first encountered feminism through Carlile in 1822–3. In 1825 he found it mooted by William Thompson, a leading Owenite who had lived briefly with Bentham and was unusual among socialists for wanting to maintain some competition in the future economic system. Mill's confidence in his father was further undermined by Macaulay's attack on the *Essay* in 1829, which assailed its reliance on supposedly universal principles of human nature, and its apparent deduction of ideas of good government from a single principle of responsibility.

In 1830–1, Mill adopted the Saint-Simonians' conception of 'organic' and 'critical' historical phases, the first where religious faith predominated, the second scepticism, and their promotion of meritocracy and restrictions on inheritance, regarding the latter as preferable to Owenite communism and equality of reward. Mill also credited the Saint-Simonians with revealing 'the very limited and temporary value of the old political economy'. He now broke from the idea that private property and inheritance were 'indefeasible facts', and freedom of production and exchange 'the *dernier mot* of social improvement', believing that the current system might precede something much better, and defined much more by equality. In 1829 he lamented that

> this idol 'production' has been set up and worshipped with
> incessant devotion for a century back, & ... the disproportionate
> importance attached to it lies at the root of all our worst national
> vices, corrupts the measures of our statesmen, the doctrines of our
> philosophers & hardens the minds of our people so as to make it

almost hopeless to inspire them with any elevation either of
intellect or of soul.   (XII.37)

This became the second great theme to dominate his thought. He
now considered writing a history of the French Revolution,
evidently giving it up because of the problem of religion; later he
contemplated a history of Greece, which also never materialized.

When revolution broke out again in France in 1830, Mill hurried
across the Channel, and, a consummate francophone, sang the
Marseillaise enthusiastically at the opera. He now hoped that
Owenite and Saint-Simonian 'anti-property' doctrines would
advance rapidly at home, if only to show the 'higher classes' 'that
they had more to fear from the poor when uneducated, than from
the poor when educated'. In Britain, too, some thought revolution
was in the air. In 1831, Mill wrote excitedly to his best friend, the
Coleridgian John Sterling, that if the peers and government
resisted parliamentary reform, 'in six months a national
convention, chosen by universal suffrage, will be sitting in
London'. The imaginary revolutionary cast himself in a key
potential role. 'If there were but a few dozens of persons safe
(whom you and I could select) to be missionaries of the great
truths in which alone there is any well-being for mankind
individually or collectively', he added, 'I should not care though a
revolution were to exterminate every person in Great Britain and
Ireland who has £500 a year. Many very amiable persons would
perish, but what is the world the better for such amiable persons?'
(He was then himself earning over £600 a year.)

This was one of several Jacobinical moments in Mill's life. Carlyle
claimed that Mill called Robespierre 'the greatest man that ever
lived', and Mill certainly felt that the 'despotism of Louis XVI
was ... bad enough to justify the French Revolution, and to palliate
even its horrors'. In 1847, he wrote that 'In England ... I often think
that a violent revolution is very much needed, in order to give that
general shake-up to the torpid mind of the nation which the

French Revolution gave to Continental Europe. England has never had any general break-up of old associations, and hence the extreme difficulty of getting any ideas into its stupid head.' In 1858, he remarked of an attempt on the life of the French emperor, Napoleon III, 'What a pity the bombs of Orsini missed their mark, and left the crime-stained usurper alive.' Regret is perhaps also evident in his 1854 remark that 'A democratic revolution is one of the most unlikely of all events in England, for English working men are never likely to rise until they are starving, and they are not likely to be starving now for generations to come.'

Mill was also becoming much more alert to national and other differences and their bearing on development. Conceding that political principles did not necessarily suit all times and places, he now posited

> That all questions of political institutions are relative, not absolute, and that different stages of human progress not only *will* have, but *ought* to have, different institutions: That government is always either in the hands, or passing into the hands, of whatever is the strongest power in society, and that what this power is, does not depend on institutions, but institutions on it: That any general theory or philosophy of politics supposes a previous theory of human progress, and that this is the same thing with a philosophy of history.   (I.186)

But while institutions were 'a question of time, place, and circumstance', for England 'the predominance of the aristocratic classes, the noble and the rich, in the English Constitution' remained 'an evil worth any struggle to get rid of'. Here Mill was very much his father's son. His later historical writing emphasized the deficiencies of medieval aristocratic ideals like chivalry, and disdain for their champions, like Edmund Burke, and doubted, like Mary Wollstonecraft, whether the gallantry towards women which supposedly resulted really indicated 'any real solicitude for their welfare'.

Around 1831, Mill found himself in 'a state of *reaction* from logical-utilitarian narrowness of the very narrowest kind, out of which after much unhappiness and inward struggling I had emerged, and had taken temporary refuge in its extreme opposite'. He remained intellectually at sea for several years, writing in 1833 that 'I am often in a state almost of scepticism, and have no theory of Human Life at all, or seem to have conflicting theories, or a theory which does not amount to a Belief'. The historian Elie Halévy later termed 'pitiful and fruitless' his 'efforts to escape from the narrow-mindedness of the Philosophical Radicals'. But this is a severe judgment. Mill's essays 'The Spirit of the Age' and 'On Genius' (both 1831) juxtapose 'stationary' and 'progressive' historical stages, and outline the role intellectual elites might play in 'transitional' ages when 'Mankind have outgrown old institutions and old doctrines, and have not yet acquired new ones.' Here Mill first mooted the theme, so central to *On Liberty*, that 'hostility to individual character' was a rising threat to humanity's progress. Like many of his generation, he was convinced that the aristocracy had lost both the ability and the will to govern. *Noblesse oblige* was a discarded concept. The 'higher classes, instead of advancing, have retrograded in all the higher qualities of mind', and this implied 'a termination to hereditary monarchy and hereditary aristocracy'. As far as intellectual ability was concerned, they had, he thought, 'certainly much less than the average share, owing to the total absence of the habit of exerting their minds for any purpose whatever'.

But who, in 'our present *transitional* condition, in which there are no persons to whom the mass of the uninstructed habitually defer', should take their place? The existing political landscape was dominated by two parties: the Tories, who usually favoured the landed interests, and the Whigs, who were more oriented towards commerce. Both remained wedded to a very restricted franchise, and to systematic bribery and corruption. The Tories in particular resisted free trade, especially in food; until 1846 substantial subsidies were paid to landlords in the form of the Corn Laws,

which kept grain prices artificially high. They were not, Mill thought, particularly interested in preserving any institutions. Instead, 'their object is to profit by them while they exist'. The Radicals struggled to attain an identity independent of merely being the left wing of the Whig party. Creating this identity now became Mill's great goal. In 1836 he defined this as 'Neo-Radicalism', meaning 'a Radicalism which is not democracy, not a bigoted adherence to any forms of government or to one kind of institutions', as well as one which included 'a utilitarianism which takes into account the whole of human nature; not the ratiocinative Faculty only…which holds feeling at least as valuable as thought, and Poetry not only on a par with, but the necessary condition of, any true and comprehensive Philosophy'.

In Parliament the Radicals had no leader, though Mill invested much effort in persuading Lord Durham to take the post. By 1837 this path was closed, and plebeian reformers began rallying around the six points of Chartism, including universal male suffrage. Mill began to doubt the Radicals' strategy, and in 1840 abandoned the political field. When the *Logic* finally appeared in 1843, Sterling reported to their friend Caroline Fox that Mill, 'brought up in the belief that Politics and Social Institutions were everything…has been gradually delivered from this outwardness, and feels now clearly that individual reform must be the groundwork of social progress'. But this still implied a leading group, now outside of politics, identified by Coleridge as a 'clerisy' and by Carlyle in *On Heroes and Hero-Worship* (1841) as an educated 'aristocracy of talent'. (Mill fell out with Carlyle during the lectures on which the book was based. He called out 'No!' when Carlyle compared 'Benthamee Utility, virtue by Profit and Loss' unfavourably to Islam, then walked out.)

Tocqueville and the later 1830s

Mill's writings in this period are dominated by four essays. Two reviews of *Democracy in America* (1835, 1840) acknowledged the

French political philosopher Alexis de Tocqueville's concept of a democratic 'tyranny of the majority' over public opinion, resulting in a downright unwillingness even to question dominant groups, and his description of equality as the new nation's guiding principle. This was a major challenge to the Benthamite orthodoxy that public opinion was incorruptible and the progress of truth inevitable. Tocqueville also identified a new, negative form of 'individualism', defined by each withdrawing from public life into 'a little circle of his own', with the result that 'Individualism, at first, only saps the virtues of public life, but, in the long run, it attacks and destroys all the others, and is at length absorbed in downright egotism'. Mill saw this negative individualism as a real danger, writing prophetically in 1835 that 'we have the greatest fear lest the classes possessed of property should degenerate more and more into selfish, unfeeling Sybarites, receiving from society all that society can give, and rendering it no service in return, content to let the numerical majority remain sunk in mental barbarism and physical destitution'. He conceded that in a commercial society, 'exclusive interest tends to fasten his attention and interest exclusively upon himself...making him indifferent to the public, to the more generous objects and the nobler interests, and, in his inordinate regard for his personal comforts, selfish and cowardly'. He acknowledged that 'the spirit of a commercial people will be...essentially mean and slavish wherever public spirit is not cultivated by an extensive participation of the people in the business of government in detail', which meant involvement in juries, local government, and other civic activities. This was a damning condemnation of the potential consequences of opulence.

Mill dissented from Tocqueville in seeing these developments as the logical outcome of commercial society as such, and only magnified by American peculiarities. This did not undermine Tocqueville's chief accomplishment, which, Mill wrote him in 1840, was to have discovered that 'the real danger in democracy, the real evil to be struggled against, and which all human

resources employed while it is not yet too late are not more than sufficient to fence off—is not anarchy or love of change, but Chinese stagnation & immobility'. But while Mill believed that America consisted of 'a republic peopled with a provincial middle class', he seems not to have conceived that this class too might become a 'sinister interest'. Privately, he could be caustic about the US, writing in 1848 that here 'the life of the whole of one sex is devoted to dollar-hunting, and of the other to breeding dollar-hunters'. His misgivings about American democracy alarmed some Radical allies at home, too, most notably Roebuck, who condemned 'ingenious plans for giving intellect her dominance'.

'On Civilisation' (1836) gave further vent to these fears by describing the present epoch as neither advancing nor progressive but 'stationary' and 'even retrograde'. People's energies were now often concentrated 'within the narrow sphere of the individual's money-getting pursuits'. This facilitated 'a moral effeminacy, an inaptitude for every kind of struggle', and a 'torpidity and cowardice', which included 'the weakening of the influence of superior minds over the multitude, the growth of charlatanerie, and the diminished efficacy of public opinion as a restraining power'. Mill concluded that 'The evils are, that the individual is lost and becomes impotent in the crowd, and that individual character itself becomes relaxed and enervated. For the first evil, the remedy is, greater and more perfect combination among individuals; for the second, national institutions of education, and forms of polity calculated to invigorate the individual character.' But he praised the fact that 'the progress of democracy is insensibly but certainly accomplishing—is gradually to put an end to every kind of unearned distinction, and let the only road open to honour and ascendancy be that of personal qualities'. Tocqueville's spirit of equality might yet eradicate traditional privilege.

Two further essays in this period, 'Bentham' (1838) and 'Coleridge' (1840), addressed 'the two great seminal minds of England in

their age', and clarified Mill's distance from orthodox Benthamism. Bentham had discerned 'more particularly those truths with which existing doctrines and institutions were at variance', while Coleridge emphasized 'the neglected truths which lay *in* them'. 'Bentham' found its subject deficient because the 'incompleteness of his own mind as a representative of universal human nature' had limited his horizons. Bentham described human nature as governed 'partly by the different modifications of self-interest, and the passions commonly classed as selfish, partly by sympathies, or occasionally antipathies, towards other beings'. All behaviour was seemingly explicable solely by the motives of seeking pleasure and avoiding pain. But to Mill this left out 'the moral part of man's nature, in the strict sense of the term—the desire of perfection, or the feeling of an approving or of an accusing conscience', as well as the

> sense of *honour*, and personal dignity—that feeling of personal exaltation and degradation which acts independently of other people's opinion, or even in defiance of it; the love of *beauty*, the passion of the artist; the love of *order*, of congruity, of consistency in all things, and conformity to their end; the love of *power*, not in the limited form of power over other human beings, but abstract power, the power of making our volitions effectual; the love of *action*.
>
> (X. 95–6)

Bentham's idea of the world was 'that of a collection of persons pursuing each his separate interest or pleasure, and the prevention of whom from jostling one another more than is unavoidable, may be attempted by hopes and fears derived from three sources—the law, religion, and public opinion'. Benthamism tended 'to make one narrow, mean type of human nature universal and perpetual, and to crush every influence which tends to the further improvement of man's intellectual and moral nature'. It did 'not pretend to aid individuals in the formation of their own character'. Indeed, it recognized 'no such wish as that of self-culture', 'the training, by the human being himself, of his affections and

will' being 'a blank in Bentham's system'. 'Man is never recognised by him', Mill reflected, 'as a being capable of pursuing spiritual perfection as an end; of desiring, for its own sake, the conformity of his own character to his standard of excellence'. Though this portrait is something of a caricature, the ideal of 'perfection' was now a key goal in Mill's system. The legacy of the 'mental crisis' required equating free will with self-culture. Here is an early plea for 'shelter for freedom of thought and individuality of character, a perpetual and standing opposition to the will of the majority'. We see too how far Mill's condemnation of Bentham's apparent obeisance to the 'despotism of Public Opinion' distanced him from both Bentham and his father. Bentham thought the 'numerical majority' could restrain the abuse of power. Mill wondered whether it was 'at all times and places, good for mankind to be under the absolute authority of the majority of themselves'. He hoped instead that 'the yoke of public opinion' could be 'tempered by respect for the personality of the individual, and deference to superiority of cultivated intelligence'.

So Benthamism failed to comprehend the 'spiritual interests of society'. Like Carlyle, the Saint-Simonians had stressed the necessity for a *Pouvoir Spirituel* ('spiritual power'), a proposal of which Mill said 'I highly approve and commend', in the hope that 'we shall one day attain, a state in which the body of the people, i.e. the uninstructed, shall entertain the same feelings of deference & submission to the authority of the instructed, in morals and politics, as they at present do in the physical sciences'. Respecting science thus naturally implied deferring to experts, not an epistemological democracy where all opinions, including the most preposterous and ill-founded, were deemed equally worthy. Nor had Bentham understood national character, and what 'causes one nation to succeed in what it attempts, another to fail; one nation to understand and aspire to elevated things, another to grovel to mean ones; which makes the greatness of one nation lasting, and dooms another to early and rapid decay'.

Bentham indeed—anticipating Margaret Thatcher and neoliberalism generally—denied that society as such existed at all. The only 'real interests' were individual, and 'community' was 'a fictitious body, composed of the individual persons who are considered as constituting as it were its members'. Mill disagreed: 'That which alone causes any material interests to exist, which alone enables any body of human beings to exist as a society, is national character', a sense of unity defined by common aspirations, identities, customs, and ways of life. He later described moral feeling as 'a natural outgrowth from the social nature of man', and argued that, 'On this basis, combined with a human creature's capacity of *fellow-feeling*, the feelings of morality properly so called seem to me to be grounded'. He returned to this issue in the *Logic*, *On Liberty*, and *Utilitarianism*.

'Coleridge' emphasized that its subject had not asked Bentham's question, 'is it true?', but rather 'what is the meaning of it?', or why social experience and tradition retain credibility and authority. Here the relation of feelings to reason was central. As in his later criticisms of the philosophers Henry Mansel and Sir William Hamilton, Mill flatly rejected Coleridge's a priori, intuitive approach to knowledge, and his claim that things could be known 'in themselves'. (Carlyle had floated a similar idea in *Sartor Resartus*, 1834.) But Mill conceded that rationalism could not wholly explain political obligation in particular. *Feelings* of allegiance and cohesion, often rooted in religion, and producing mutual sympathy and common interest, played a major role in political stability, which Benthamism's focus on self-interest could not fathom. Coleridge posited that two principles, permanence and progression, needed to be balanced in any society. Mill disagreed that the landed interest should be invariably identified with the former and the commercial interest with the latter. The contrast, he thought instead, should be between 'the contented classes & the aspiring—wealth & hopeful poverty—age & youth—hereditary importance & personal endowments'.

Coleridge promoted his own version of the Saint-Simonians' 'spiritual power' or intellectual elite, which he called a 'clerisy'. In 1831, Mill defined this as 'all who are capable of producing a beneficial effect on their age and country as teachers of the knowledge which fits people to perform their duties and exercise their rights, and as exhorters to the right performance and exercise of them'. He agreed that 'an endowed class for the cultivation of learning' should exist. (The *Principles* later suggested that governments 'by means of endowments or salaries' might maintain a 'learned class'.) Coleridge recognized that the empirical method led to atheism, a direction Mill was happy to take, though not publicly. Much of the debate about epistemology, in fact, was a proxy war really aimed at assessing the grounds and reasonableness of religious belief, with the underlying world of 'things-in-themselves' corresponding to 'faith' and the empirical world to scientific observation.

Mrs Taylor appears

Mill's youth was apparently bereft of romance. Sensuality seems never to have disturbed him. Here his experience, like Bentham's, hardly represents humanity as a whole. In 1830, however, Mill met the love of his life, Harriet Taylor. Aged 23, she was 'a beauty and a wit, with an air of natural distinction, felt by all who approached her . . . a woman of deep and strong feeling, of penetrating and intuitive intelligence, and of a most meditative and poetic nature'. Unfortunately she was married to someone else. Soon he was dining at her house, her unusually understanding husband, John Taylor, absenting himself. They began thinking and writing together; Taylor's biographer, Jo Ellen Jacobs, describes their joint efforts in terms of a 'collaborative self' (see Figure 4).

It would be 20 years before John Taylor died and, after an appropriate interval of mourning, they married in 1851. The period between brought all the opprobrium of Victorian middle-

4. Harriet Taylor (1807–58).

class intolerance for what was in fact an utterly innocent
friendship devoid of sexual contact. (In 1831, her diary recorded
that 'Our dining together and long conversations will not, can not,
be replaced by more intimate acts.' We know now that her
husband had infected her with syphilis.) Among Mill's friends
their relationship was 'the familiar talk of all the circle'. Carlyle
first called Harriet 'a living romance-heroine, of the clearest
insight, of the royallest volition; very interesting', but came, like

33

Mill's father, to disapprove entirely of her, and referred to her disdainfully as 'Platonica'. Some close friends, notably Roebuck, warned him of the consequences of impropriety. Mill suffered greatly from such gossip, and his health was affected. Never the life of the party, he withdrew from 'society' during much of the second half of his life. Latterly her daughter, Helen Taylor, became his chief helpmate. This isolation, however, probably allowed him greater independence of thought than a more sociable life might have done.

Until her death in 1858, in any case, this void was to Mill more than adequately filled by Harriet. Her influence on him was profound. Mill saw her as an 'apostle of progress' who helped lift him out of the narrow Benthamism of his youth. He exhausted the range of superlatives in praising her; one was that the poet Shelley 'was but a child compared with what she ultimately became'. He later claimed that all his main works after meeting her, excepting the *Logic* but including the *Principles*, were a 'joint product'. *On Liberty*, 'more directly and literally our joint production than anything else which bears my name', invoked her 'great thoughts and noble feelings' and 'all but unrivalled wisdom'. 'What was abstract and purely scientific was generally mine', he noted, 'the properly human element came from her: in all that related to the application of philosophy to the exigencies of human society and progress, I was her pupil'. In particular, all speculation about

> changes in the present opinions on the limits of the right of
> property and which contemplate possibilities, as to the springs of
> human action in economical matters which had only been affirmed
> by Socialists and in general fiercely denied by political economists;
> all this, but for her, would either have been absent from my writings
> or would have been suggested much more timidly and in a more
> qualified form.   (I. 256)

How should these claims affect our perception of Mill? Generations of writers, particularly the more conservative-leaning,

have lamented Mill's apparent weakness and emotional susceptibility in his deference to Harriet, and alternatively blamed her, Mill, his father, and utilitarianism in general. Scholars remain divided as to the nature and extent of her influence. Smitten Mill certainly was, and willing—far too willing to her critics—to modify his positions at her behest. The historian Goldwin Smith felt that 'Mill's hallucination as to his wife's genius deprived him of all authority wherever that came in'. Roebuck said 'she had the art of returning his own thoughts to himself, clothed in her own words, he thought them hers, and wondered at her powers of mind, and the accuracy of her conclusions'. Alexander Bain thought her capable of 'intelligently controverting his views than by merely reproducing them in different language'. Mill's brother George regarded her as clever and remarkable, but hardly as accomplished as Mill supposed. To the journalist and critic Leslie Stephen, 'her influence was rather upon his emotions than upon his intellect', and it was 'impossible to attribute to Mrs. Mill any real share in framing his philosophical doctrines', although she 'encouraged him to a more human version of the old Utilitarian gospel'. Much later the conservative historian Gertrude Himmelfarb condemned her 'vanity, arrogance, pettiness, affectation, complacency, willfulness, petulance, domestic tyranny'.

This controversy remains important because some of Mill's ideas were substantially modified by Harriet's direct intervention, notably respecting communism, about which he remained more doubtful, and socialism, to which he warmed. The first edition of the *Principles* (1848) treats this subject quite sceptically. The second (1849) approaches it far more optimistically, while the third (1852) portrays socialism virtually as a viable alternative to capitalism. Here, to Himmelfarb, as on the subject of liberty, 'his wife had evidently urged upon him a more extreme position than he would have taken on his own'. The most damning evidence supporting this view is a letter from Mill to Harriet in 1849, while the *Principles* were being revised, stating that 'the objections as now stated to Communism are valid: but if you do not think so,

I certainly will not print it, even if there were no other reason than the certainty I feel that I never should long continue of an opinion different from yours on a subject which you have fully considered'. The *Principles'* most famous chapter, 'The Probable Futurity of the Labouring Classes'—to Mill its most influential and original section, which distinguished it 'from all previous expositions of Political Economy that had any pretentions to be scientific'—he described as 'entirely due to her', including the suggestion of 'the extreme imperfection of the book without it'. Much of the technical side of the *Principles*, Mill acknowledged, was an exposition of Ricardo (see Figure 5). But this chapter went far beyond the horizons of earlier generations of economists. Here Harriet shaped what Mill described as 'the only substantial changes of opinion that were yet to come', which

> related to politics, and consisted, on one hand, in a greater
> approximation, so far as regards the ultimate prospects of
> humanity, to a qualified Socialism, and on the other, a shifting of
> my political ideal from pure democracy, as commonly understood
> by its partisans, to the modified form of it, which is set forth in my
> *Considerations on Representative Government.*

There were other sources of his alteration in opinions. Mill's most comprehensive biographer, Michael Packe, asserts that 'the violent change in Harriet's mind produced by the events of 1848 was a complete surprise to him'. But Mill reacted viscerally to the new French government following the February revolution, writing that 'I feel an entireness of sympathy with them which I never expected to have with any political party'. In a burst of enthusiasm he stated that 'If France succeeds in establishing a republic and reasonable republican government, all the rest of Europe, except England and Russia, will be republicanised in ten years, and England itself probably before we die'. These views are consistent with the trajectory of Mill's radicalism, and now led him to study French socialism with care. Mill equally credited Harriet with saving him from 'a tendency towards over-government both social and political'.

5. **David Ricardo (1772–1823).**

The *System of Logic* (1843)

By 1840 the prospect of a new Radical party had receded, and Mill
returned to his larger intellectual projects. The first of two works
which defined his mid-Victorian reputation, the seemingly
narrowly focused *Logic*, which examines the 'art of reasoning', is
disingenuously titled. It addresses the so-called Enlightenment

project insofar as it aims to clarify how knowledge is grounded, and whether 'laws' govern human behaviour in the same manner as natural phenomena. It argues that the Absolute—'things-in-themselves'—cannot be known, and that all knowledge instead is relative, thus undermining beliefs rooted in superstition and ignorance. Mill's chief target is intuitionism, which depicts the real world as reflecting ideas already existing in the mind. His approach is sometimes called 'naturalistic' insofar as, by contrast to, say, Kant's theologically grounded system, the supernatural plays no role in it. So reasoning has an end: demonstrating these assumptions, and reducing all knowledge to experience.

The *Logic* thus paved the way for *On Liberty*'s defence of freedom of enquiry. Crucial for Mill was the method by which 'proofs' were determined, and establishing their degrees of probability, which were dependent on observable 'laws' rooted in experience to which no exceptions existed. In cases like belief in God or the soul's immortality (to Bentham, 'extra-experimental belief'), the *Logic* aimed to undermine intuitive claims. In social and political thought it rejected the common assumption that 'human nature and society will for ever revolve in the same orbit, and exhibit essentially the same phenomena'. Here, thus, the 'empirical law' of 'the progressive change in the condition of the human species' had priority. This was not the best of all possible worlds: an imaginative leap enabled an appreciation of something better.

All attempts at unique or special knowledge, especially the theological, were thus suspect. Nonetheless, Mill hedged his bets carefully, describing miracles as possibly resulting from a supernatural cause, and thus still consonant with general laws of causation, though evidence for them was less reliable. This put paid to the hopes Carlyle, who in 1831 called Mill a 'partial disciple of mine', had that he was a 'new mystic', on the basis of the 'Spirit of the Times' essays, or that Coleridge too entertained of gaining a new follower. Place wrote that Mill had 'made great progress in becoming a German metaphysical mystic'. But Mill remained

resolutely in the tradition of Locke, Hartley, and his father. The universe was governed by ascertainable general laws and was wholly comprehensible on rational grounds. 'The most incessant occupation of the human intellect throughout life is the ascertainment of truth', he reiterated in 1865. The 'Enlightenment Project' had been reaffirmed.

In book 6, 'The Logic of the Moral Sciences', Mill explained how the 'art' of politics rested on a 'science' of politics. He rejected both pure induction, such as Macaulay proposed, and pure deduction (Bentham) as inadequate, the first because it could not be generalized to large groups, the second because it rested on too narrow a conception of human nature. Induction was 'the process by which we conclude that what is true of certain individuals of a class is true of the whole class, or that what is true at certain times will be true in similar circumstances at all times'. Deduction, the interpretation of general propositions, was only possible once laws based upon experience had been identified. Mill's alternative, the 'Inverse Deductive Method', used observable historical facts to provide 'empirical laws of society' which were confirmable by recourse to known psychological laws. 'Logic' showed both how we reason and how opinions were formed. These often derived, he thought, from feelings, 'the impression which [someone] derived from what he saw or heard', rather than the rational assessment of evidence governed by laws, which involved rising above the feeling attached to a judgment.

But if behaviour was governed by laws, how far could individuals alter the circumstances around them and be said to possess 'free will'? We recognize Mill's 1827 problem. Unsurprisingly, his favourite chapter of the *Logic*, 'Of Liberty and Necessity' (book 6, chapter 2), summarized the 'train of thought which had extricated me from this dilemma'. He told his friend Caroline Fox to read it first, followed by the account of 'Ethology' (book 6, chapter 5), the 'science of the formation of character...produced in conformity to those general laws, by any set of circumstances, physical and

moral', particularly respecting different national characters. These remain the two chapters most readers return to today. Many necessitarians made 'the eternally recurring error of confounding Causation with Fatalism'; that is, of assuming that the operation of general laws of behaviour left no scope for individual choice, which implied inevitability or predetermination. Here, as in his assessment of Sir William Hamilton's philosophy (1865), Mill rejected as 'Asiatic fatalism' the view that individual desires were always superseded by divine powers. A second variation on the theme, 'Modified Fatalism', he identified with Owenism's claim that 'our actions are determined by our will, our will by our desires, and our desires by the joint influence of the motives presented to us and of our individual character; but that, our character having been made for us and not by us, we are not responsible for it, nor for the actions it leads to, and should in vain attempt to alter them'. All fatalism was encouraged by theology, which demanded faith in mere superstition, and threatened what Mill termed 'a main portion of the Art of Living—that of not believing except on sufficient evidence'.

Mill's sense of his own identity, and what he wanted to be, required rejecting both positions. So did his wish to reconcile a general system of causal determination with the possibility of free choice. At least to a degree, we might be responsible for our actions. Positing a free will, 'being capable of choice', wrote one of his leading interpreters, the intellectual historian Isaiah Berlin, 'is what Mill seems to me to have cared about most of all'. 'Human volitions and actions' were 'necessary and inevitable' insofar as all behaviour resulted from existing causes. Free will was essential to any conception of autonomy and progress, yet seemingly violated the idea of the universality and 'uniformity of sequence' of causal laws. How could these be reconciled? What is often called a compatibilist response, for instance by the philosopher Harry Frankfurt, attempts such a rapprochement in suggesting that while an act may be unavoidable, we may remain morally responsible. Certainly, to Mill, we might in certain circumstances

claim to master the impulses and desires which otherwise shape our behaviour. Moral freedom consisted in at least recognizing, if not actually exercising, such mastery. (For to will is not to act.) 'We are exactly as capable', Mill asserted, 'of making our own character, *if we will*, as others are of making it for us.' Thus,

> this feeling, of our being able to modify our own character *if we wish*, is itself the feeling of moral freedom which we are conscious of. A person feels morally free, who feels that his habits or his temptations are not his masters, but he theirs: who even in yielding to them knows that he could resist; that were he, for any reason, desirous of altogether throwing them off, there would not be required for that purpose a stronger desire than he knows himself to be capable of feeling. (VIII. 841)

'To be conscious of free-will', Mill thought, 'must mean, to be conscious, before I have decided, that I am able to decide either way'. 'Virtue' meant that an individual's 'desire to do right, and his aversion to doing wrong, are strong enough to overcome, and in the case of perfect virtue, to silence, any other desire or aversion which may conflict with them'. This was part of what constituted 'character', that is, both crafting our own personality and choosing virtue over vice. 'Self-command', which we alone can teach ourselves, captures both aspects. Mill added, in 1868: 'And hence it is said with truth that none but a person of confirmed virtue is completely free.'

This was a reassuring but still unsatisfactory argument. (And terms like 'perfect' and 'completely' make relativist critics nervous.) Immense variations exist in the circumstances which foster such consciousness and permit the exercise of such 'freedom'. In the vital case of the market, for example, the workman, Mill wrote in 1830,

> is not a free agent. A workman once entered into the employment of a master is not free; his poverty, the lowness of his wages, *the law*

of settlement, render it impossible for him to leave his service, to remain one, two, or three weeks idle, to travel to other parishes in search of an employer; and he is obliged, therefore, to submit to the exactions and frauds of an oppressive and fraudulent master.

A more useful question, then, would be: *under what circumstances* can we be said to possess 'free will'? And a more plausible answer would be: when we are capable of fulfilling our desires, for we cannot have 'free choice' where our desires are merely a fantasy, not capable of being acted on, or are impeded by others. And we cannot have 'free will' to choose our own character where the very conception of so doing is absent, or the building blocks of another type of character are missing. To insist otherwise is delusional.

Mill felt that he now had a handle on the relation between free will and self-culture. Less successful was his exposition of 'Ethology', 'the science which corresponds to the art of education'. This was driven by the need to identify and then create the types of personality corresponding to what Mill regarded as superior forms of society, and was again a response to his own mental crisis. Here he acknowledged that the 'Germano-Coleridgian school', which included the German philosopher Johann Gottfried Herder and the French historian Jules Michelet, had done more to illuminate 'various elements of human culture and the causes influencing the formation of national character' than previous efforts, by emphasizing the unique trends in every culture. Mill's wider aim was to counter the 'Bentham School', who 'founded their general theory of government on one comprehensive premise, namely, that men's actions are always determined by their interests', and to explain how other motives might be fostered, and how a 'common system of opinions' developed which underpinned national and other forms of cohesion. 'Political Ethology' aimed to reveal 'the causes which determine the type of character belonging to a people or to an age', an effort which he admitted was, among all the branches of social science, 'the most

42

6. **Auguste Comte (1798–1857).**

completely in its infancy', but which focused initially on Mill's favourite theme, 'progression in the intellectual convictions of mankind'. He was here much inspired by the French philosopher Auguste Comte's tracing of the development of religious opinion from the theological through the metaphysical to the future positive stage, which would witness the full flourishing of the scientific spirit (see Figure 6). He aimed to write further on ethology, but abandoned the task in 1844, turning instead to composing the *Principles*, which was full of ethological observations and ambitions.

Mill never lost interest in the subject, but there were good reasons for his failure to take this ill-fated project further. Establishing general laws to explain particular varieties, reasoning first from the latter, was ponderous. There was also a mass of prejudices to

cut through respecting 'national character'. Mill considered that, 'Of all vulgar modes of escaping from the consideration of the effect of social and moral influences on the human mind, the most vulgar is that of attributing the diversities of conduct and character to inherent natural differences', as in the case of blaming Irish poverty on the indolence of 'the Celtic Race'. So other explanations had to be sought. Ethology fascinated but eventually defeated him, though in 1854 he and Harriet were still sketching out 'Differences of character (nation, race, age, sex, temperament)'.

What drove these reflections was the linkage between ideal societies and ideal character types. In rephrasing the problem of 1827, Mill aimed to assess how specifically 'English' qualities might be tempered by qualities or traits dominant in other nations, particularly France. The problem was explaining the variations, ranking the various qualities which might be deemed desirable or reprehensible, and determining their causes. Here Mill exhibited some apparent inconsistency. On the one hand, he praised at various points the 'striving, go-ahead character' of Britain and the US in particular, highlighting its energy, ingeniousness, and hostility to 'stationariness'. This was clearly associated with competitiveness, the work ethic, and action generally. On the other, he conceded much to the Latin and Mediterranean, and especially the French, temperaments, writing Comte in 1846 that 'I have stood for quite some time in a kind of open opposition to the English character, which arouses my animosity in several respects; and all in all, I prefer the French, German or Italian character'. His admiration for the French was revealed in a striking comment on 'the contrast between the frank sociability and amiability of French personal intercourse, and the English mode of existence in which everybody acts as if everybody else (with perhaps a few individual exceptions) was either an enemy or a bore'. He wrote the Saint-Simonian Gustave D'Eichthal that 'the very worst point in our national character' was 'the disposition to sacrifice every thing to accumulation, & that exclusive & engrossing selfishness which accompanies it'.

This was linked to an English tendency to overwork, which was also dual edged. Mill wrote in 1843 that 'An Englishman is a more hard-working animal than a Frenchman or a German: he throws more of his energy, more (we may say) of his life, into his work'. As a result,

> Before a Continental operative can be as steady a workman as an Englishman, his whole nature must be changed: he must acquire both the virtues and the defects of the English labourer; he must become as patient, as conscientious, but also as careworn, as anxious, as joyless, as dull, as exclusively intent upon the main chance, as his British compeer. He will long be of inferior value as a mere machine, because, happily for him, he cares for pleasure as well as gain.   (XXIV. 838–9)

Mill often complained that the English were obsessed with 'what they call their advancement in life'. He thought this made them overly conservative, and lamented 'how invariably the instinct of the English people is on the side of the status quo. In all foreign wars, revolutions, &c., English opinion is sure to be against the side, be it king or people, that seems to be attempting to alter an existing order of things.' The reason for this was that

> The English, of all ranks and classes, are at bottom, in all their feelings, aristocrats. They have some conception of liberty, & set some value on it, but the very idea of equality is strange & offensive to them. They do not dislike to have many people above them as long as they have some below them. And therefore they have never sympathized & in their present state of mind never will sympathize with any really democratic or republican party in other countries.
>
> (XV. 553)

This implies that the legacy of 1827 was an ideal of character which rejected the mere 'machine' and aimed at a balance of work and leisure, wealth and culture, and self-interest and empathy for the less fortunate. Economic Man might be replaced by a more

fully human personality. Here Mill's insights and foresight remain highly relevant.

Character and the public good

Mill's engagement with ethology reflected a concern with 'character' which continued for the rest of his life, and followed logically from the 'crisis' and his subsequent concern with free will, as well as from utilitarianism generally. But 'character' meant more than balancing work and leisure. Morally and politically, it meant accepting public duty as a rule in life—the jurist John Austin said he had 'an equal devotion to the two cardinal points of Liberty and Duty'. Self-mastery was vital to achieving this. Mill evidently thought that we are basically disposed in this direction; in 1867 he stated that 'If you take an average human mind while still young, before the objects it has chosen in life have given it a turn in any bad direction, you will generally find it desiring what is good, right, and for the benefit of all.' The rest could be accomplished by the 'almost boundless' power of education. Thus, 'if that season is properly used to implant the knowledge and give the training which shall render rectitude of judgment more habitual than sophistry, a serious barrier will have been erected against the inroads of selfishness and falsehood'. The specific goal of this process he later described as 'nobility of character'. For an opponent of aristocracy, to whom 'nobility' implied voluptuousness, waste, profligacy, and vice, it was an odd choice of words. Clearly Mill, echoing Aristotle, meant by it generosity, self-control, dignity, self-sacrifice, and altruism.

Pursuing the public good was thus a dominant principle for Mill; the great Victorian sociologist Herbert Spencer noted of him, 'How entirely his public career has been determined by a pure and strong sympathy for his fellow-men—how entirely this sympathy has subordinated all desires for personal advantage.' But Mill puzzled long as to how to make this serve as a regular source of motivation. Here, perhaps, his classical training came to the fore.

Grote called him a 'Greece-intoxicated man', for Mill regarded the Greeks as 'the greatest people who have yet appeared on this planet' because of 'the powers and efforts required to make the achievement'. Thus, 'an average Athenian was a far finer specimen of humanity on the whole than an average Englishman'. When Bentham once asked him what the most important event in English history was, the young Mill deftly replied, 'The Battle of Marathon' (490 BCE), when Greece repelled Persia and defended that combination of political freedom and rational enquiry which to Mill defined civilization. The Romans played a role here too. In 1855 he wrote Harriet of his 'extreme admiration' for the Stoic Marcus Aurelius. Originally a Greek philosophy, Stoicism stressed above all the need to rise above the mere love of pleasure and fear of pain, and emphasized that only the wise were truly free. This implies an ideal type for Mill. An empirical method would deduce the laws which produced its formation, and then ascertain where parallel conditions lay elsewhere and how they might be adapted. Modern democracies lacked a pervasive sense of the public good. But this could be remedied. The *Principles* asserted that 'Mankind are capable of a far greater amount of public spirit than the present age is accustomed to suppose possible. History bears witness to the success with which large bodies of human beings may be trained to feel the public interest their own.' 'There will', Mill thought, 'never be honest or self-restraining government unless each individual participant feels himself a trustee for all his fellow citizens and for posterity', adding, 'Certainly no Athenian voter thought otherwise.'

The *Logic* suggested that public virtue was attainable where 'the cultivation of an ideal nobleness of will and conduct, should be to individual human beings an end, to which the specific pursuit either of their own happiness or of that of others (except so far as included in that idea) should, in any case of conflict, give way'. As Mill stressed in 1867, 'The test of right on the happiness principle is not the pleasure of doing the act which is declared to be right, but the pleasurable or painful consequences to mankind which

would follow if such acts were done.' Social pressure helps motivate us to prefer the common good. But the strength of the 'social feeling' was often insufficient. As *Utilitarianism* put it,

> The deeply-rooted conception which every individual even now has of himself as a social being, tends to make him feel it one of his natural wants that there should be harmony between his feelings and aims and those of his fellow creatures...This feeling in most individuals is much inferior in strength to their selfish feelings, and is often wanting altogether.

The Religion of Humanity

Could religion play a role in promoting moral duty? Mill felt grateful that he had never had religion forced on him as a child. His father, he wrote, 'looked upon religion as the greatest enemy of morality', 'by radically vitiating the standard of morals; making it consist in doing the will of a being on whom it lavishes the most servile phrases of adulation but whom in sober truth it depicts as eminently hateful'. Christians (and others) were routinely intolerant of non-believers, whose cause would be central to the claims for freedom of opinion defended in *On Liberty*. Could faith and reason be reconciled? From adolescence onwards this remained a central question in all Mill's work.

Much of Mill's treatment of religion was filtered through his engagement with Auguste Comte (1798–1857), whom he termed in 1843 'by far the first speculative thinker of the age'. Saint-Simon's former secretary, Comte was best known for his threefold scheme of succession of historical as well as analytical stages, the theological, metaphysical, and positive, a kind of secular millenarianism in which reason triumphs. His sociology identified a need for both Order and Progress, or Social Statics and Social Dynamics. This chimed well with Mill's reading of the Saint-Simonians and Coleridge, and was adapted in the *Principles* and *Considerations* in particular. Mill agreed with Comte that 'the

moral and intellectual ascendancy, once exercised by priests, must in time pass into the hands of philosophers'. But he rejected Comte's proposal that they should be 'organized into a kind of corporate hierarchy' like the Catholic Church. Comte's insistence on women's intellectual inferiority Mill also regarded as wholly unacceptable. He eventually broke from Comte on this issue in 1846, and denounced Comte's 'pedantocracy', or government by philosophers, as likely to 'be composed, not of great thinkers, but simply of scholars or of scientists lacking true originality'. Later Mill rejected the governmental scheme proposed in Comte's *Système de Politique Positive* (1851–4) as 'the completest system of spiritual and temporal despotism which ever yet emanated from a human brain'.

Mill was, however, much more sympathetic to Comte's suggestion that a Religion of Humanity, revering not gods but a pantheon of human heroes, might supplant Christianity as reason finally laid superstition to rest. Comte aimed, Mill said, at cultivating 'to the highest point the sentiments of fraternity with all our fellow beings, past, present, and to come', by a 'veneration for those past and present who have deserved it, and devotion to the good of those to come'. The stress here was on feeling. Comte valued 'the systematic and earnest inculcation of the purely *subordinate* role of the intellect as the minister of the higher sentiments'. This Mill thought a grand achievement. Comte answered what was in effect Coleridge's problem: how to crystallize the loyalty of large groups, but without embracing theological dogma. The 'central idea' of Comte's philosophy, 'replacing the religious with the scientific point of view', was indeed a key ambition in Mill's main works, linking the *Logic*, *On Liberty*, the *Considerations*, and *The Subjection of Women*.

Such discussions could still be very dangerous, and Mill remained reluctant to appear a religious sceptic, much less an outright atheist. In a transitional age unbelief had to emerge gradually. He wrote John Sterling in 1831 that in Britain infidels 'ought not in

my opinion to form a part of the national *clerisy*, for their exertions might 'make men worse instead of better by shaking the only firm convictions & feelings of duty which they have, without having even a remote chance of furnishing them with any effectual substitute'. But in more advanced France the Saint-Simonians might well serve the cause. In 1844 Mill told Comte that the 'time has not yet come when we in England shall be able to direct open attacks on theology, including Christian theology, without compromising our cause. We can only evade the issue by simply eliminating it from all social and philosophical discussion and by passing over all questions pertaining to it on our agenda.' Mill rejoiced when Alexander Bain abandoned his faith after reading Comte, but advised the latter (in 1845) that 'an attempt to publicly set up an antireligious school...would frighten the public, broach premature discussions, at least in England, and would probably lend new strength to religious reaction'. Most of the time Mill confined himself to suggesting limited reforms, like abolishing established churches and paid clergy, and removing religious teaching from schools and colleges. Yet occasional outbursts revealed his resentments bubbling to the surface. In treating Sir William Hamilton's philosophy, famously, he proclaimed that 'I will call no being good, who is not what I mean when I apply that epithet to my fellow-creatures; and if such a being can sentence me to hell for not so calling him, to hell I will go'. If he rests there today, the devil surely has a worthy adversary.

Chapter 3
Political economy and social philosophy, 1845–59

In the third phase of his intellectual growth, commencing in the late 1830s, Mill wrote that he and Harriet 'completely turned back from what there had been of excess in my reaction against Benthamism'. This meant that 'We were now much less democrats than I had been, because so long as education continues to be so wretchedly imperfect, we dreaded the ignorance and especially the selfishness and brutality of the mass: but our ideal of ultimate improvement went far beyond Democracy, and would class us decidedly under the general designation of Socialists.' Aspiring to 'Democracy', he had once thought chimerical the prospect of 'removing the injustice…that some are born to riches and the vast majority to poverty', and hoped that 'by universal education, leading to voluntary restraint on population, the portion of the poor might be made more tolerable'. Now, the *Autobiography* relates,

> While we repudiated with the greatest energy that tyranny of
> society over the individual which most Socialistic systems are
> supposed to involve, we yet looked forward to a time when society
> will no longer be divided into the idle and the industrious; when the
> rule that they who do not work shall not eat, will be applied not to
> paupers only, but impartially to all…The social problem of the
> future we considered to be, how to unite the greatest individual
> liberty of action, with a common ownership in the raw material of

the globe, and an equal participation of all in the benefits of combined labour. (I. 239)

This perspective, as much Harriet's as John's, dominates the *Principles*, and renders its extremely ambitious contribution to modern thought distinctive and enduring.

Embracing co-operation

In the mid-1840s, as Mill abandoned the ethology project for political economy, he began engaging seriously with an approach to socialism through the co-operative movement, which had grown partly out of Owenism. This allowed him to project ideals of equality and economic justice through an apparently practical means of overcoming capitalism's tendency to undermine both, with none of the demands and renewed social pressure which communal living arrangements involved. An important essay, 'The Claims of Labour' (1845), announced Mill's conversion to this ideal:

> If, on a subject on which almost every thinker has his Utopia, we might be permitted to have ours; if we might point to the principle on which, at some distant date, we place our chief hope for healing the widening breach between those who toil and those who live on the produce of former toil; it would be that of raising the labourer from a receiver of hire—a mere bought instrument in the work of production, having no residuary interest in the work itself—to the position of being, in some sort, a partner in it. (IV. 382)

Just what this meant has been much debated, however. Leslie Stephen assumed that for Mill co-operation meant 'simply the joint effort of independent individuals. Competition is assumed to remain in full force.' This implies a 'free' market in labour and capital. But Mill used the term 'co-operation' in several senses. Concerning the working classes, he insisted that 'It is not co-operation between a few persons to join for the purpose of

making a profit from cheap purchases, by which one, two, or more might benefit. Co-operation is where the whole of the produce is divided.' And his proposed restrictions on inheritance and plea for more equal systems of distribution, we will see, clearly imply something quite different from unregulated capitalism. The broader principle of private property, that each may do what they wish with their own, was not accepted by Mill after the late 1820s. Its application, he noted in 1836, would mean that 'in all Europe at no distant date, we see property entirely concentrated in a small number of hands'. Co-operation would prevent this, and Mill was optimistic about its progress. In 1863, he wrote that he did not 'take a gloomy view of human prospects. Few persons look forward to the future career of humanity with more brilliant hopes than I do', while adding that he saw 'many perils ahead, which unless successfully avoided could blast these prospects'.

The *Principles of Political Economy* (1848)

The *Principles*, with its crucial subtitle, *With Some of Their Applications to Social Philosophy*, exhibits Mill's colours as a visionary. The book was also his greatest popular success, reaching 32 editions in the 19th century and as many in the 20th, making him the leading writer on the subject since Adam Smith. The narrower economics of the work generally restated Ricardo, albeit with greater clarity, and championed free trade and an international division of labour as opposed to protectionism and national autarky. Opulence was seen as the aim of modern societies, which required capital accumulation. This brought expanding industry and employment. The advent of new wants stimulated the desire to labour and to accumulate. Concentrating employment in productive rather than unproductive labour increased social output. A rising standard of living generally resulted. But universal opulence was not automatic; in rich countries a 'very large' number lived 'by pillaging or overreaching other people'. Mill's broader aim was to reduce this class, and to promote greater economic and social equality generally.

He condemned profligacy, waste, and idleness, and praised frugality and abstinence for both rich and poor alike.

There is surprisingly little here on industrialization, the blight of urban growth, or the effects of factory conditions on the labour force, however. We are not in the same world as *Das Kapital*. Yet Mill found fault with much in the existing system. Like Ricardo, he initially insisted that rising profits implied decreasing wages, and vice versa. In 1869, he finally broke from the Ricardian 'wages fund' theory. He now conceded that trades' unions could improve wages, and were 'an indispensable auxiliary of labour', though 'healing the feud between capitalists and labourers' through co-operation might eventually 'supersede trade unions'. Mill also doubted whether technological innovation actually improved workers' lives, writing that it was 'questionable if all the mechanical inventions yet made have lightened the day's toil of any human being', as they had 'enabled a greater population to live the same life of drudgery and imprisonment, and an increased number of manufacturers and others to make fortunes'. (Marx added in *Capital*: 'Mill should have said, "of any human being not fed by other people's labour", for there is no doubt that machinery has greatly increased the number of distinguished idlers.') He also regarded the system of competition to be imperfect, warning, like Smith, that the fewer the competitors, the less competition would result. But this had to be balanced against the principle that 'wherever competition is not, monopoly is'.

Modern readers often find three main features of the *Principles* to be novel and appealing. Much of what distinguished the book lay in Mill's application of what he called a 'Philosophy of Life' to economics, and in assigning to 'art' the governance of the 'science' which explained how economies functioned. 'Science', he wrote in 1844, 'is a collection of truths; art a body of rules, or directions for conduct. The language of science is, This is, or, This is not; This does, or does not, happen. The language of art is, Do this; Avoid

that.' The science of political economy was narrowly concerned with accumulating wealth, and prior to Mill had achieved a reputation for deducing (im)moral axioms from the iron laws of the market. As in later neoliberalism, it often insisted that these laws were as inviolable as that of gravity. But there was more to life than this, and again Mill revisited the problem of free will. 'In England', he thought, 'it is not the desire of wealth that needs to be taught, but the use of wealth, and appreciation of the objects of desire which wealth cannot purchase, or for attaining which it is not required.' Unlike the laws governing wealth production, its distribution was 'a matter of human institution solely', and 'mankind, individually or collectively, can do with them as they like'. Hence art ought necessarily to determine humanity's best ends. What in 1867 he called 'the emancipation of political economy' involved going beyond 'what they call economical laws, demand & supply for instance, as if they were laws of inanimate matter, not amenable to the will of the human beings from whose feelings, interests, & principles of action they proceed'.

Second, the *Principles* was defined by Mill's increased sympathy for a 'qualified' socialism, in the sense of more collectivist approaches to property ownership, which was evident by the third edition (1852). The first edition said it was 'not easily conceivable' that 'a country of any large extent could be formed into a single "Co-operative Society"', while conceding that 'a country might be covered with small Socialist communities, and these might have a Congress to manage their joint concerns', which was Owen's plan. But in 1850 Mill worried that in such communities,

> the yoke of conformity would be made heavier instead of lighter; that people would be compelled to live as it pleased others, not as it pleased themselves; that their lives would be placed under rules, the same for all, prescribed by the majority; and that there would be no escape, no independence of action left to any one, since all must be members of one or another community.

The system of private property might thus be 'compatible with a far greater degree of personal liberty'. But with Harriet to hand his reservations dissipated rapidly, and he now seemingly shifted ground. Such schemes generally supposed, Mill stated, that 'The direction of the labour of the community would devolve upon a magistrate or magistrates, whom we may suppose elected by the suffrages of the community, and whom we must assume to be voluntarily obeyed by them.' Besides greater social equality and democracy, another advantage lay in the motive to labour: 'A factory operative has less personal interest in his work than a member of a Communist association, since he is not, like him, working for a partnership of which he is himself a member.'

Mill nonetheless still warned that 'it is an admitted condition of the Communist scheme that all shall be educated', adding that 'this being supposed, the duties of the members of the association would doubtless be as diligently performed as those of the generality of salaried officers in the middle or higher classes'. His chief objection to socialism thus lay in 'the unprepared state of mankind in general, and of the labouring classes in particular; their extreme unfitness at present for any order of things, which would make any considerable demand on either their intellect or their virtue'. A lengthy correspondence with Harriet over this period reveals that Mill held his ground, still doubting at vital points:

You say 'if there were a desire on the part of the cleverer people to make them perfect it would be easy'—but how to produce that desire in the cleverer people? I must say I think that if we had absolute power tomorrow, though we could do much to improve people by good laws, & could even give them a very much better education than they have ever had yet, still, for effecting in our lives anything like what we aim at, all our plans would fail from the impossibility of finding fit instruments. To make people really good for much it is so necessary not merely to give them good intentions & conscientiousness but to unseal their eyes—to prevent

self flattery, vanity, irritability & all that family of vices from
warping their moral judgments as those of the very cleverest people
are almost always warped now.   (XIV. 19)

By 1852, Mill was committed to much greater egalitarianism than
anything Bentham envisioned. The 'great end of social
improvement', he suggested, should be 'a state of society
combining the greatest personal freedom with that just
distribution of the fruits of labour which the present laws of
property do not even propose to aim at'. This destination, he wrote
in 1865, in a classic statement of his unique liberal paradigm, lay
'not in some new form of dependence but in the emancipation of
the dependent classes—more freedom, more equality, more
responsibility of each person for himself'. The hybrid system he
envisioned, as expressed in 1869, was the 'plan of industrial
partnership', which was 'highly worthy of encouragement, as
uniting some of the advantages of co-operation with the principal
advantages of capitalist management'. Thus it might be possible
'ultimately to arrive at a state of industry in which the workpeople
as a body will either themselves own the capital, or hire it from its
owners'.

Mill still insisted that 'Communism at its best' should be
compared 'with the régime of individual property, not as it is, but
as it might be made. The principle of private property has never
yet had a fair trial in any country; and less so, perhaps, in this
country than in some others.' A reformed capitalism, with the
principle of reward for work universalized, ensuring a 'guarantee
to individuals of the fruits of their own labour and abstinence',
might well prove superior. The laws of property, Mill thought,

> have never yet conformed to the principles on which the
> justification of private property rests. They have made property of
> things which never ought to be property, and absolute property
> where only a qualified property ought to exist. They have not held
> the balance fairly between human beings, but have heaped

impediments upon some, to give advantage to others; they have purposely fostered inequalities, and prevented all from starting fair in the race.

Private property offered a powerful incentive to produce. Mill was fond of quoting the agricultural writer Arthur Young to the effect that 'the magic of property' 'turns sand into gold'. Peasants, in particular, with security of tenure, could transform a 'bleak rock' into a garden.

The chief impediment here was inheritance, which gave some the 'fruits of the labour and abstinence of others...without any merit or exertion of their own'. This was, however, 'not of the essence of the institution, but a mere incidental consequence, which, when it reaches a certain height, does not promote, but conflicts with, the ends which render private property legitimate'. Here Mill exposed the core of his theory of justice. 'It is unjust', he argued, 'to tax a person because, by his own savings, he acquires a large fortune, and to tax him in a larger proportion than if he had squandered more and saved less; but there is no injustice in taxing persons who have not acquired what they have by their own exertions, but have had it bestowed them in free gift'. As expressed in the 7th edition of the *Principles* (1871), the solution was limiting inheritance to 'the means of comfortable independence'. Bain thought this would 'pull down all large fortunes in two generations'.

This public statement implies some inconsistency, since a universal duty to labour seems to be superseded. Privately, however, Mill was, or perhaps became, more radical, writing in October 1871, *after* the last edition of the *Principles* to be published under his supervision had gone to press, that 'I would lay a heavy graduated succession duty on all inheritances exceeding that moderate amount, which is sufficient to aid but not to supersede personal exertion'. This chimes well with an earlier remark—again indicating a break from his father—that 'I have

even ceased to think that a leisured class, in the ordinary sense of the term, is an essential constituent of the best form of society'. Was this the effect of the short-lived experiment in workers' control in the Paris Commune (1871) and the revival of discussions of socialism? The unfinished 'Chapters on Socialism' was under way, and this indicates a more radical conclusion to this work. Had Mill returned to what he recognized as the Saint-Simonian principle of his youth, that 'no one who does not work either with head or hands, shall be allowed to eat'? We cannot be sure.

Linked to these discussions was Mill's clear opposition to any absolute right of private property in land, based on the principle that 'No man made the land. It is the original inheritance of the whole species.' He also delineated a wide range of cases where state intervention might be justified, including protecting the young, regulating hours of labour and the quality of goods sold, and educating and assisting the poor. Where monopolies occurred naturally, as in the case of railways, the state could rightfully regulate prices, though Mill insisted that 'in no case does it seem to me admissible that the Gov^t should *work* the railways. If it became proprietor of them it ought to lease them to private companies.' But there were other areas where public, and especially local and municipal, authority might use property for the general well-being. He wrote Herbert Spencer that

> I cannot help thinking that public gardens should be the property of the town, in order that they may be free to all without payment: and though I do not think so of public baths, yet in order to foster the taste for them, and render them ultimately a profitable private speculation, I should not object to their being experimentally provided by public authority.

Mill applied these principles in his writings on Ireland in particular, urging land reform and fixity of tenure, even with land held in common, and rent, which he increasingly regarded as an 'unearned increment', paid to the state. During the Famine of

1846–7 he urged that waste lands be converted to peasant properties, imagining that Ireland might be remade in the image of Norway or Switzerland. Later he bitterly regretted that 'the profound ignorance of English politicians and the English public concerning all social phenomena not generally met with in England (however common elsewhere) made my endeavours an entire failure'.

Mill's general maxim in such cases was that state intervention was justified where 'people require artificial help, to enable them afterwards to help themselves', for instance in granting loans to improve working-class housing. These were substantial inroads into the right of property. 'The State', Mill wrote in 1832, 'is at liberty to modify the general right of property as much as it likes; to new-model it altogether, if the public interest requires it.' This might include, he later wrote of works of art, a 'right to require that those who possess such treasures should either open their galleries to public view, or at least lend the contents from time to time for the purpose of exhibition; and should allow to artists under reasonable restrictions regular access to them for the purpose of reproduction or of study'. In 1865, it was even reported that 'Mill said he thought no pictures ought to be kept by individuals but national works of art should be given up to the nation for the public to enjoy & in the same way men with parks ought to admit the public'.

The third distinctive element of the *Principles* was its overt neo-Malthusianism. Population control was closely linked to more extensive state interference. In 1848 Mill wrote of claims to a 'right to work' in France that 'I think it likely that society will ultimately take the increase of the human race under a more direct controul than is consistent with present ideas', adding that 'an unlimited "droit au travail" for all who are born, as well as many other things, would not be the chimeras which they seem to be in the present state of opinion & feeling'. At Harriet's urging, Mill again insisted that only by restraining population growth

could long-term benefit for the working classes be expected. He pointed to countries with low birth rates and a high standard of living for the peasantry, like Norway and parts of Switzerland. He posited that in some circumstances there was a 'justification for converting the moral obligation against bringing children into the world who are a burthen to the community, into a legal one'. In 1848 he stressed that while 'every one of the living brotherhood of humankind has a moral claim to a place at the table provided by the collective exertions of the race, no one of them has a right to invite additional strangers thither without the consent of the rest'. Consequently, 'All persons…should abdicate the right of propagating the species at their own discretion and without limit', though 'before this solution of the problem can cease to be visionary, an almost complete renovation must take place in some of the most rooted opinions and feelings of the present race of mankind'. Mill also suggested that respecting overpopulation, 'Communism' was 'precisely the state of things in which opinion might be expected to declare itself with greatest intensity against this kind of selfish intemperance'. (One of Mill's modern editors remarks that this sounds 'more like Orwell's bad dream of 1984 than the sentiments of the author of the essay *On Liberty*!!') Even in later years Mill could also appear harsh in his attitudes towards the poor. Asked in 1868 about poor-houses, he reiterated his belief that it was just to separate young married persons, though not the elderly, and invoked the principle 'that for young people and for able-bodied people the workhouse should be a place of discomfort…since the people themselves are often very much to blame for bringing themselves into a position in which they require relief'. But unlike Malthus he did consider birth control to be an option for the poor, rather than merely abstinence.

Fourth, Mill's treatment of the 'stationary state' made the *Principles* a distinctive, and now distinctively modern, book. The Scottish philosopher John MacCunn calls Mill's discussion of this issue 'surely one of the most cheerful forecasts that ever came from philosophic pen'. Here again we see the triumph of art over

science. A condition of no growth was a bogey for earlier political economists. But Mill saw it as an 'ultimate point' of social progress, where

> society would exhibit these leading features: a well-paid and affluent body of labourers; no enormous fortunes, except what were earned and accumulated during a single lifetime; but a much larger body of persons than at present, not only exempt from the coarser toils, but with sufficient leisure, both physical and mental, from mechanical details, to cultivate freely the graces of life.   (III. 755)

Here too we have a sense of Mill, whose love of the countryside, botany, and wandering were central to his leisure, as a proto-ecological thinker. In 1865 he asserted that 'There is now almost no place left on our own planet that is mysterious to us, and we are brought within sight of the practical questions which will have to be faced when the multiplied human race shall have taken full possession of the earth (and exhausted its principal fuel).' This condition Mill described as 'greatly preferable to the present'.

Fifth, central to the novel outlook of the *Principles* was the chapter 'On the Probable Futurity of the Labouring Classes'. About this the economist J. E. Cairnes wrote that it was 'no exaggeration to say [that it] places a gulf between Mill and all who preceded him, and opens an entirely new vista to economic speculation'. Written at Harriet's instigation, it projected a society where no class was 'not labouring', with co-operation 'putting an end to the division of society into the industrious and the idle, and effacing all social distinctions but those fairly earned by personal services and exertions'. Mostly against Carlyle, Mill denied that work was 'a good in itself', writing that there was 'nothing laudable in work for work's sake ... On the contrary, the multiplication of work, for purposes not worth caring about, is one of the evils of our present condition.' He queried 'How many of the so-called luxuries, conveniences, refinements, and ornaments of life, are *worth* the labour which must be undergone as the condition of producing

them?' This vision of life beyond the work ethic is more relevant than ever.

Equality and class

The ideal of equality championed in the *Principles* must be weighed against Mill's much better known commitment to liberty. The jurist Albert Venn Dicey thought that here his views belonged 'to the school rather of Rousseau than of Bentham'. But Mill agreed with Bentham in 1848 that equality, 'though not the sole end, is one of the ends of good social arrangements', and that 'a system of institutions which does not make the scale turn in favour of equality, whenever this can be done without impairing the security of the property which is the product and reward of personal exertion, is essentially a bad government—a government for the few, to the injury of the many'. Occasionally Mill reveals a Platonic vein on this subject, as in the comment that 'It is only the high-minded to whom equality is really agreeable. A proof is that they are the only persons who are capable of strong and durable attachments to their equals; while strong and durable attachments to superiors or inferiors are far more common and are possible to the vulgarest natures.' (Remember that Plato's Guardians in the *Republic* were communists.) Yet equality was the basis of the best life; as he commented elsewhere, 'In my estimation the art of living with others consists first & chiefly in treating & being treated by them as equals.' This is very much the spirit of *The Subjection of Women*, which presents his most impassioned defence of the principle.

Mill's approach to class involved the collision of two principles: a growing commitment to equality, and recognizing that striving for wealth entailed permitting its accumulation to some degree, thus fostering inequality. In 1825, Mill did not object to 'a class of rich men, I care not how rich, if they become so no otherwise than by the natural operation of the laws of property'. By 1831 he modified this, stating that

the wealth of a country is upon a footing most favourable to human happiness, just in proportion to the number of persons whom it enables to obtain, by their bodily and mental exertions, a comfortable subsistence; while on the contrary, a further increase of the wealth of particular individuals beyond this point, makes a very questionable addition to the general happiness; and is even, if the same wealth would otherwise have been employed in raising other persons from a state of poverty, a positive evil. (XXII. 249)

Mill continued to insist that a reasonable reward for the loan of capital was justified, and viewed capitalists as adequately recompensed by a 3–4 per cent return on investment. Limiting inheritance would prevent too great an accumulation of wealth. Like Owen, Mill tended to see the chief enemy of the working classes as the middlemen who enhanced the price of goods:

It is the enormous number of mere distributors who are not producers that really eat up the produce of labour, much more than the mere profits of Capital, which, in a great majority of cases, are not more than a reasonable equivalent for the industry which created the capital and the frugality which prevents it from being squandered. The direction in which I look for the greatest improvement in Social economy, is the suppression of the vast number of middlemen who share among themselves so large a proportion of the produce of the country, while the service they render though indispensable, might be as well and better performed by a tenth part of their number. (XV. 864)

Mill also had a somewhat idealized view of competition, noting in 1865 that 'to carry on business at a loss in order to ruin competitors is not fair competition. In such a contest, if prolonged, the competitors who have the smallest means, though they may have every other element of success, must necessarily be crushed through no fault of their own.' Such cases might 'justly be called the tyranny of capital', and should be avoided. But many would see this as the normal working of the capitalist system.

So, too, Mill denied in 1848 that a capitalist could 'take advantage of the labourer's necessities, and make his conditions as he pleases. He could do so, undoubtedly, if he were but one. The capitalists collectively could do so, if they were not too numerous to combine, and act as a body. But, as things are, they have no such advantage.' For an enemy of aristocracy, Mill seems curiously inattentive to the possibility of a new aristocracy of capitalists. Perhaps he was reluctant to embrace the theory of social degeneration this implied, which contradicted his belief that 'the general tendency is, and will continue to be, saving occasional exceptions, one of improvement; a tendency towards a better and happier state'. In 1835, he wrote that 'the important matter is not *by whom* we are governed, but *how*:—with due securities for their being properly qualified, we should not complain, although the whole legislature were composed of *millionnaires*'. By 1865, however, when running for Parliament, he conceded that he was 'deeply convinced that there can be no Parliamentary Reform worthy of the name, so long as a seat in Parliament is only attainable by rich men, or by those who have rich men at their back'. As for Marx, only a distribution of economic power could alter this tendency.

Chapter 4
The values of *On Liberty* (1859)

In 1854, Mill told his friend George Grote that he 'was cogitating an essay to point out what things society forbade that it ought not, and what things it left alone that it ought to control'. His aim was to offer a single principle explaining what should be in each category, thus cutting through prejudice, and particularly religious bias, leading Mill to suspect that the work would likely 'be called an infidel book'. The *Principles* had described 'a circle around every individual human being' which no one should overstep, as a 'part of the life of every person who has come to years of discretion, within which the individuality of that person ought to reign uncontrolled either by any other individual or by the public collectively'. The core argument was restated in 1850: 'No order of society can be in my estimation desirable unless grounded on the maxim, that no man or woman is accountable to others for any conduct by which others are not injured or damaged.'

The book made a surprising impact. In 1917, John Morley recalled that 'I do not know whether then or at any other time so short a book ever instantly produced so wide and so important an effect on contemporary thought as did Mill's On Liberty in that day of intellectual and social fermentation'. It had, Mill wrote soon after its publication, 'much more success, and has made a greater impression, than I had the smallest expectation of'. He rightly

thought it 'likely to survive longer than anything else that I have written', terming it 'a kind of philosophic text-book of a single truth, which the changes progressively taking place in modern society tend to bring out into ever stronger relief: the importance, to man and society, of a large variety in types of character, and of giving full freedom to human nature to expand itself in innumerable and conflicting directions'. The result is a veritable bible of modern identity, not only proclaiming the toleration of difference and diversity but championing them. It remains one of the best handbooks we have for judging the propriety of everyday moral activity (see Figure 7).

On Liberty has five main aims. The first is to protect progressive minorities, who play a leading role in social advancement, from the 'tyranny of the prevailing opinion and feeling', and particularly the intolerance of evangelical Christians, whom Mill thought in the ascendant. The second is to defend private life from unwarranted oppression by others, by generalizing an ancient maxim usually used in medicine, *primum non nocere*—'do no harm'—through a distinction between 'self-regarding' and what are often called 'other-regarding' acts, though Mill does not use the latter term, preferring 'social'. The third is to promote the principle that maximizing liberty was the best means of fostering self-responsibility and accounting for one's own actions. This was central to Mill after 1827, and was the essence of having free will; he denies early on that the essay concerns the latter subject, but it does. We are also led to understand that enjoying this sense of sovereignty and freedom makes us happy. (But so can renouncing responsibility to 'God' or 'fate'.) The fourth is to describe individuality, understood as self-development, or 'the conformity of our character to ideal perfection according to some particular standard', as the *Logic* phrased it, as key to both personal and social development. The fifth is to define the principle that 'each person is the only safe guardian of his own rights and interests'. This Mill subtly qualifies by implying that others sometimes know our interests better than we do.

ON

LIBERTY

BY

JOHN STUART MILL.

LONDON:
JOHN W. PARKER AND SON, WEST STRAND.
M.DCCC.LIX.

7. *On Liberty* title page (1859).

These five aims are not always compatible, and conflicts between them may not be easily soluble. In each area Mill defends what are today termed both 'negative' and 'positive' ideas of liberty; that is, we should be as free as possible from the coercion of others, but freedom should also be used for our self-development in specific directions, particularly towards virtue, self-mastery, and rationality, wherein the help of others may be vital. A negative liberty reading is frequently encountered among scholars, and even more the wider public. But Mill's bold introductory comment that 'The only freedom which deserves the name, is that of pursuing our own good in our own way, so long as we do not attempt to deprive others of theirs, or impede their efforts to obtain it', is quite deceptive. Some see it as defending autonomy, or anarchic or libertarian self-rule. Carefully considered, however, this is a much less simple theory of liberty than we might initially assume. Mill's leading modern commentator, the philosopher Alan Ryan, insists that '*Liberty* is not an essay about doing your own thing; it is an essay about finding the best thing and making it your own'. This only fully makes sense when we read the chapter on 'Individuality' alongside the essay 'Utilitarianism', and realize that liberty should point us towards 'higher' and 'nobler' pleasures and forms of character.

What is today the most famous paragraph in all Mill's works outlines the 'very simple principle' being defended:

> that the sole end for which mankind are warranted, individually or collectively, in interfering with the liberty of action of any of their number, is self-protection, That the only purpose for which power can be rightfully exercised over any member of a civilized community, against his will, is to prevent harm to others. His own good, either physical or moral, is not a sufficient warrant. He cannot rightfully be compelled to do or forbear because it will be better for him to do so, because it will make him happier, because, in the opinions of others, to do so would be wise, or even right...The only part of the conduct of any one, for which he is amenable to society,

is that which concerns others. In the part which merely concerns himself, his independence is, of right, absolute. Over himself, over his own body and mind, the individual is sovereign. (XVIII. 233–4)

The central phrase, 'the sovereignty of the individual', Mill acknowledged he owed to the American individualist and former Owenite Josiah Warren. It is easily misunderstood as an unqualified vindication of 'negative liberty'; that is, allowing individuals to do what they like so long as minimal 'harm' provisions are not violated. It is often taken as a complete rejection of 'paternalism', which Mill defined in 1844 as the view among the labouring classes 'that it is the business of others to take care of their condition, without any self control on their own part—& that whatever is possessed by other people, more than they possess, is a wrong to them, or at least a kind of stewardship, of which an account is to be rendered to them'. Clearly, being left to our own devices, choices and judgment *is* an important part of Mill's scheme. The principle of liberty, he stresses, 'requires liberty of tastes and pursuits; of framing the plan of our life to suit our own character; of doing as we like, subject to such consequences as may follow: without impediment from our fellow-creatures, so long as what we do does not harm them, even though they should think our conduct foolish, perverse, or wrong'. Making such choices is what defines our freedom, and proves our free will, the exercise of which is central to our moral growth.

The purpose of protecting progressive minorities is to push back against the growing conformity of modern society. Now, Mill worried,

from the highest class of society down to the lowest, every one lives as under the eye of a hostile and dreaded censorship. Not only in what concerns others, but in what concerns only themselves, the individual or the family do not ask themselves—what do I prefer? or, what would suit my character and disposition? or, what would allow the best and highest in me to have fair play, and enable it to

grow and thrive? They ask themselves, what is suitable to my
position? what is usually done by persons of my station and
pecuniary circumstances? or (worse still) what is usually done by
persons of a station and circumstances superior to mine? I do not
mean that they choose what is customary, in preference to what
suits their own inclination. It does not occur to them to have any
inclination, except for what is customary. Thus the mind itself is
bowed to the yoke: even in what people do for pleasure, conformity
is the first thing thought of; they like in crowds; they exercise choice
only among things commonly done.   (XVIII. 264–5)

From the outset, Mill's argument hinges on how we define 'harm
to others'. This is not straightforward. Physical harm we all
understand. What about the degrees of coercion or absence of
voluntariness/'consent' in many acts, some subtle, some overt,
which might produce less obvious forms of 'injury' or 'damage'? Is
not depriving others of freedom itself 'harm'? What proportion of
our acts are really 'voluntary', when even our desire for pleasure is
often instinctual (or group-driven) rather than rationally,
individually, and autonomously conceived? We do many things we
would rather not do, but are, effectively, forced to do, like working
for low wages, or doing what stupid bosses or politicians demand.
We buy and even think things because people pay advertisers to
persuade us to—is this 'voluntary'? We are clearly back to, and
cannot escape from, the free will question. And what about the
psychological wounds people may claim we inflict when our
criticism of their opinions 'insults', 'offends', or denigrates their
beliefs? Should 'harm' here be defined entirely subjectively?

Mill's answer is suggestive, but not definitive or exhaustive. He
variously paraphrases forms of 'harm' as involving damage to the
rights or interests of others. Since 'no person is an entirely isolated
being', too, our behaviour may 'seriously affect' those close to us.
Think of suicide, apparently the ultimately 'self-regarding' act, but
devastating for those close to the victim. But Mill insists that only
when we 'violate a distinct and assignable obligation to any other

person or persons' does an act become non-self-regarding, or 'social', and at least 'amenable to moral disapprobation', if not legal interference. (In this way for a hermit, lacking such obligations, suicide might be justifiable, but for someone with a family, it could not be.)

Violating a 'distinct and assignable obligation' is the nearest Mill comes to a precise definition of harm. This implies that many harms may be tolerated, or subject to disapprobation, mostly by moral suasion or group pressure, itself potentially coercive even if not harmful; there may be a fine line between 'persuading' and 'compelling'. The phrase seems oriented primarily towards familial duties and legal obligations. One telling example Mill gives is that if 'a man, through intemperance or extravagance, becomes unable to pay his debts, or, having undertaken the moral responsibility of a family, becomes from the same cause incapable of supporting or educating them, he is deservedly reprobated, and might be justly punished; but it is for the breach of duty to his family or creditors, not for the extravagance'. So too, 'No person ought to be punished simply for being drunk; but a soldier or a policeman should be punished for being drunk on duty.' And 'making himself drunk, in a person whom drunkenness excites to do harm to others, is a crime against others'. The principle here seems clear: 'Whenever, in short, there is a definite damage, or a definite risk of damage, either to an individual or to the public, the case is taken out of the province of liberty, and placed in that of morality or law.' But this does not tell us what cases fall into each category.

The boundary between self-regarding and non-self-regarding acts remains very blurred. But the harm principle takes the government, as well as nosy neighbours, out of a large part of private life, certainly out of the bedroom, if not the library, permitting a wide range of activities then condemned in Britain, often by severe punishment. Bentham's very liberal views on homosexuality were not known until recently, but the spirit of non-interference in all such matters is clearly supported by Mill. It

would be a long time before public opinion caught up. Henry Sidgwick later commented that 'Mill's doctrine is certainly opposed to common sense: since (e.g.) it would exclude from censure almost all forms of sexual immorality committed by unmarried and independent adults'. But Mill's plea for non-interference clearly remains as relevant today.

'Liberty' is, however, not the only issue in play here. Mill is juggling a number of interwoven potential first principles, namely liberty, individuality, progress, and utility. If he is to be a systematic utilitarian, the last has logical priority. Doubtless feeling autonomous does make us happier. But Mill claims his defence of liberty is based on 'utility in the largest sense, grounded on the permanent interests of man as a progressive being', 'progressive' here meaning chiefly an evolution from seeing happiness as one's own pleasure and in terms of lower-order pleasures, towards a more refined and virtuous outlook. Here progress seems to drive utility, which must ever be on the move, and liberty has as one part of its end, indeed possibly its chief aim, individuality. What kind of social order will best promote these is not at issue here, though it is evident, as Alan Ryan insists, that more happiness might be achieved with less liberty, and vice versa. Mill's editors complain that his 'increased sympathy for socialism is not evident in *On Liberty*', as if this pointed to a lapse in this sympathy, though we know the volume was a joint John/Harriet production. But it does not. Mill simply presumed his readers were acquainted with the *Principles*' views on socialism.

Freedom of thought and discussion

'Of the Liberty of Thought and Discussion' is logically the first chapter of *On Liberty*, for no society can progress without the greatest possible freedom of opinion. Echoing Bentham, who believed political tyranny often rested on claims of infallibility of judgment, James Mill had contended that publicity was 'the great instrument for creating and applying the moral sanction, the

approbation and disapprobation of mankind', and that 'All other publicity is feeble and of little worth compared with that of the *Press*'. His essay on the liberty of the press confidently asserted that 'Every man, possessed of reason, is accustomed to weigh evidence, and to be guided and determined by its preponderance.' With a confidence which eludes us today, he added that, 'When various conclusions are, with their evidence, presented with equal care and with equal skill, there is a moral certainty, though some few may be misguided, that the greater number will judge aright.'

On Liberty follows suit, albeit with greater reservations about the inevitable rectitude of majority opinion. Mill famously states that, 'If all mankind minus one, were of one opinion, and only one person were of the contrary opinion, mankind would be no more justified in silencing that one person, than he, if he had the power, would be justified in silencing mankind.' But tolerating other people's views does not mean that we cannot criticize them. Many reasons exist to doubt the validity of opinions. What we believe mostly derives from our immediate environment, and so results not from reasoned argument but upbringing, and often group and social pressure. According to Mill's theory of knowledge, now restated, respecting religious views, 'the same causes which make him a Churchman in London, would have made him a Buddhist or a Confucian in Pekin'. This provocatively implied, of course, a subversively relativist challenge to the idea that the truth-content of any religion was greater than any other. But merely following the customary and habitual in all areas was precisely what Mill was trying to avoid. The examined, self-reflective life is the ideal: Mill challenges us to scrutinize and challenge all our ideas, and especially those we most cherish. 'If the cultivation of the understanding consists in one thing more than in another', *On Liberty* insisted, 'it is surely in learning the grounds of one's own opinions.' And, it might be added, learning to judge on the basis of opinion rather than feeling, for too many reasoned on the basis of 'sympathies and antipathies' rather than 'interests', and when 'lost in the crowd' their opinions were often uncritical. No opinion was

so sacred as to be unquestionable, and to scrutinize all, particularly where religion was concerned—many of Mill's examples concern the persecution of 'heretics' and blasphemers—was a moral duty.

The test of truth was thus the essence of progress. Like his father, Mill presumes that, presented with true opinions, rational beings will relinquish weaker or false ones, and truth will conquer error. This is an admirable but faulty premise, since our inability and even willingness to distinguish falsehood and propaganda from truth is sadly limited, as the age of mass media and 'fake news' all too amply demonstrates. Self-delusion and the corruption of interest and ambition hinder or distort our perceptions. There is no 'free market' in opinions, since numerous propaganda machines run by sinister interests constantly repeat lies which assume the appearance of truths, and consciously sustain stupidity and promote ignorance and prejudice. And while everyone wants freedom for their own opinions, we often denigrate those with whom we markedly disagree. Mill's doctrine demands that we must tolerate much that offends us, even when the offence is deliberate. For offence is not 'harm'. Truth can only be ascertained by the collision of opinions, and sometimes collisions hurt. This is the price of progress. Diversity of opinion necessarily remained a good 'until mankind are much more capable than at present of recognizing all sides of the truth'. Obviously Mill hoped that opinions might coalesce around what the most thoughtful and intelligent believed. Until then, opinions simply had to slug it out, in what was evidently a pretty unequal struggle in which a contempt for 'experts' might well win out.

Individuality

Mill promoted the idea of the self-formation of character after his mental breakdown. The short essay on genius of 1831 stressed the necessity of encouraging intellectual development. Tocqueville's account of American democracy painted a frightening portrait of

majority opinion, whose impact Mill thought could not long be avoided in Europe. In 1835, he wrote of Tocqueville that 'He dreads lest all individuality of character, and independence of thought and sentiment, should be prostrated under the despotic yoke of public opinion', and quoted his observation that 'I am acquainted with no country in which there reigns, in general, less independence of mind, and real freedom of discussion, than in America'. The *Principles* reiterated that 'those manifold unlikenesses, that diversity of tastes and talents, and variety of intellectual points of view', 'by bringing intellects into stimulating collision, and by presenting to each innumerable notions that he would not have conceived of himself, are the mainspring of mental and moral progression'. In 1851, Mill warned again, in writing, that 'changes effected rapidly & by force are often the only ones which in given circumstances would be permanent', and that 'the stupidity & habitual indifference of the mass of mankind would bear down by its dead weight all the efforts of the more intelligent & active minded few'.

Chapter 3 of *On Liberty*, 'Of Individuality, As One of the Elements of Well-Being', develops these observations into a full-blown, dramatic, and radical theory of the benefits of individuality to each person and to progress generally. 'In proportion to the development of his individuality', we are told, 'each person becomes more valuable to himself, and is therefore capable of being more valuable to others.' Individuality means acting according to a 'person's own character', rather than allowing 'the traditions or customs of other people' to be one's 'rule of conduct'. Mill's use of the concept represents the working out of the problem of self-cultivation and free will from 1827 onwards. Mental growth results from challenging conformity and established custom: 'He who does anything because it is the custom, makes no choice.' In a bold injunction to eccentricity and rebelliousness, Mill insists, citing Wilhelm von Humboldt, that creativity, genius, and 'individual vigour and manifold diversity' combine as 'originality'. Here diversity becomes an end in itself, as

well as a means of enriching others. Like truths, the very proliferation of a richness of character types hastens us towards choosing the better ones.

Active choice is central to this scheme. A mechanical, unthinking life is less than fully human. Compared to those who let others 'choose his plan of life for him', Mill argues, 'He who chooses his plan for himself, employs all his faculties. He must use observation to see, reasoning and judgment to foresee, activity to gather materials for decision, discrimination to decide, and when he has decided, firmness and self-control to hold to his deliberate decision.' Someone possesses 'character' whose 'desires and impulses are his own—are the expression of his own nature, as it has been developed and modified by his own culture': 'If a person possesses any tolerable amount of common sense and experience, his own mode of laying out his existence is the best, not because it is the best in itself, but because it is his own mode.' The same could be said—ethology rears its head—for entire nations, which might possess originality or, like 'the whole East', suffer under 'the despotism of custom'. In both cases we must avoid mediocrity 'and character inert and torpid, instead of active and energetic'. We are not far off here, John Burrow suggests, from the language of civic humanism or civic moralism. 'Individuality' assists the well-being of all by promoting progress and public liberty, from which all benefit, though it may undermine the values of the majority. Yet those who possess self-mastery and self-control may well be most prone, or most often called upon, to sacrifice their own happiness for that of the majority, for this is Mill's chief test of virtue. Freedom here clearly means self-determination, the activity which is walled off by prohibitions against unnecessary social interference in our actions. But liberty is also not so much doing what we want, or simple autonomy, as doing what is good for us and for society—a considerable difference. We are still 'free' to do what we want—but we ought to want what aids humanity's development, not what degrades it or ourselves. For this makes us unfree, both individually and collectively.

Mill concedes that not everyone can attain individuality equally, or even acknowledge its value. Many will follow those few who originate new trends or ideas and are the motor-force of progress. The 'initiation of all wise or noble things comes and must come from individuals; generally at first from some one individual', so that the 'honour and glory of the average man is that he is capable of following that initiative; that he can respond internally to wise and noble things, and be led to them with his eyes open'. (John Morley agreed that 'the multiplication and elevation of types of virtuous character, and the practical acceptance of these types by the general sentiment', were the goals here.) All, however, could be encouraged to try 'different experiments of living', doubtless partially a euphemism covering his relationship with Harriet, with a view to producing 'varieties of character', whose diversity was every bit as necessary as that of opinion. Mill gives as one, pretty daring example, Mormon polygamy, attacks on which were disguised as a 'civilizade'. Here he insisted that 'I am not aware that any community has a right to force another to be civilized'. This implies a considerable plea for value pluralism, whose limits are unclear, though the burden of proof seems to rest on custom to justify the continuance of any practice. Here Mill's commitment to progress is daring and distinctive. But he means communities within already supposedly 'civilized' states: the principle does not hold for empires or conquered and colonized indigenous peoples.

Individuality, then, Mill now proclaimed, was 'quite the chief ingredient of individual and social progress' as well as 'one of the principal ingredients of human happiness'. But desiring it also potentially pits us against social mores on many occasions, with predictable results, namely unhappiness when the majority punishes our deviance. (Remember John and Harriet!) The injunction to rebel which these claims represent also understates our strong desire to belong to groups, and our sometimes desperate willingness to conform, even to sacrifice our integrity, in order to gain their approval. But this was the price to be paid for avoiding 'stationariness' and the 'despotism of custom'. Society had

already 'now fairly got the better of individuality'. There was no time to lose.

How does the prioritizing of individuality affect Mill's philosophical system? To the 20th-century political theorist John Plamenatz, Mill, 'without knowing it, abandons utilitarianism' in asking 'what more or better can be said of any condition of human affairs than that it brings human beings themselves nearer to the best thing they can be', adding that 'Nothing could be less utilitarian than the spirit of this question.' But as early as 1834 Mill had responded:

> Though I hold the good of the species (or rather of its several units) to be the *ultimate* end, (which is the alpha & omega of my utilitarianism) I believe with the fullest Belief that this end can in no other way be forwarded but by...each taking for his exclusive aim the developement of what is best in *himself*. (XII. 207-8)

The family and the right of propagation

Even today the most controversial part of *On Liberty* concerns an apparently deeply private issue: child-bearing. In 1854 Mill had written to a correspondent that

> what any persons may freely do with respect to sexual relations should be deemed to be an unimportant and purely private matter, which concerns no one but themselves. If children are the result, then indeed commences a set of important duties towards the children, which society should enforce upon the parents much more strictly than it now does. (XXVII. 664)

Alexander Bain said that Mill told his friend Grote that the book, while arguing against many social restraints, might suggest new ones, but said nothing more, with the latter commenting: 'I instantly divined what the new restraints would be.' The issue, ignored by generations of Mill commentators, including many

focused specifically on Mill's views on liberty, was again birth control. The *Principles* had noted that various European states required evidence of the ability to support a family before permitting marriage. Mill now stated: 'The laws which, in many countries on the Continent, forbid marriage unless the parties can show that they have the means of supporting a family, do not exceed the legitimate powers of the State: and whether such laws be expedient or not (a question mainly dependent on local circumstances and feelings), they are not objectionable as violations of liberty.' He reiterated in 1865 that 'restrictions on marriage, or on any other human action when so conducted as to be directly injurious to others than the agents themselves, do not appear to me objectionable on the principle of Liberty'.

The message here, as in 1848, was that social progress required such restraint. But such interference was not for the individual's good, for this the harm principle could not permit: it was for the good of society. So too Mill insisted, as the French provisional government struggled to frame new welfare measures, that

> one of the most important and responsible of moral acts, that of giving existence to human beings, is a thing respecting which there scarcely exists any moral obligation, and in which no person's discretion ought on any pretence to be interfered with: a superstition which will one day be regarded with as much contempt, as any of the idiotic notions and practices of savages. (XX. 350)

The third edition of the *Principles*, however, asserted that 'There would be no need … of legal sanctions, if women were admitted as on all other grounds they have the clearest title to be, to the same rights of citizenship with men.' Gender equality would bring about voluntary restraint in family size, and thus avoid such a substantial interference in individual liberty. An interim solution, hinted at in 1845, was that providing the poor with welfare could be tied to their voluntary restriction of marriage and stringent penalties for illegitimate births. In 1848 Mill restated this:

The practical result of the whole truth might possibly be, that all persons living should guarantee to each other, through their organ the State, the ability to earn by labour an adequate subsistence, but that they should abdicate the right of propagating the species at their own discretion and without limit: that all classes alike, and not the poor alone, should consent to exercise that power in such measure only, and under such regulations, as society might prescribe with a view to the common good.   (XX. 350)

All such restrictions, however, were hampered by the problem of class. Mill elsewhere defended his views in suggesting that 'he never had said that the working classes had not as much right as the higher classes, but that they had no more right. Neither had a right to have more children than they could support and educate.' But this implied the poor had less 'right' to bear children simply because they could support fewer than the rich. A blanket prohibition was deeply unfair; we have moved little distance from the same problem today. This implies that Mill was not a methodological individualist in his ethics: the family is the basic unit of society, and familial obligation is central to Mill. The example shows that the 'libertarian' or negative liberty reading of Mill is largely erroneous. Commentators point to Mill's description in an 1871 letter of the central theme of the book as 'l'autonomie de l'individu', without noting that Mill was as concerned with the limits of this autonomy as its defence in principle. (He also added in this letter that 'dans ceux de nos actes qui touchent directement aux intérêts d'autrui, il faut à mon sens une autre règle, celle de l'intérêt général' (The general interest should be the rule respecting all acts which affect others).)

Applications

On Liberty's final section, 'Applications', excludes trade from the harm principle, so forcing the sale of opium on the Chinese at gunpoint is justified, though poisons should be labelled. Those who fail to support their children through sheer idleness can be

compelled to labour. Mill baulks at regulating prostitution and gambling. A general responsibility to educate the young is recognized, though Mill argues that the state should not undertake this itself, as this tends to 'moulding people to be exactly like one another'. He introduces three general principles aimed at restricting the scope of governmental interference: where things are better done by individuals; where individual mental development is better served; and where governmental power may be unduly augmented.

Mill concedes some types of paternalism. If, for instance, we see someone trying to cross a bridge which has been deemed unsafe, we may prevent them, 'for liberty consists in doing what one desires, and he does not desire to fall into the river'. This principle might be very widely extended, for neither do we desire to become sick, to go hungry, or to be injured. Today we consider examples like using seat-belts, wearing masks in a pandemic, being vaccinated, or not smoking indoors, where individual rights and the social good may appear to clash, but where paternalistic intervention usually meets with public approval, especially where failing to protect ourselves may harm others.

On Liberty offers us another perspective on the legacy of the mental crisis, the *Logic*'s discussion of free will, and Mill's idea of 'character'. The ideal of 'Christian morality', writes Mill, 'is negative rather than positive; passive rather than active; Innocence rather than Nobleness; Abstinence from Evil, rather than energetic pursuit of good; in its precepts (as has been well said) "thou shalt not" predominates unduly over "thou shalt"'. Mill wants us to be energetic, strong, spontaneous, vigorous, and original. 'Pagan self-assertion' thus counterbalances Christian self-denial, and assists 'self-formation'. Most of Mill's critics, however, felt that he veered too far in the direction of individual freedom, and was unduly alarmed about the decline of individuality. In the chief contemporary reply to *On Liberty*, *Liberty, Equality, Fraternity* (1873), the lawyer James Fitzjames

Stephen dismissed Mill's central distinction between self-regarding and non-self-regarding acts, and, guided by his own experience in India, counselled a vigorous state-led suppression of immorality. He thought Mill had underestimated the value of fear and coercion in guiding human conduct. Nor was Mill a consistent utilitarian in *On Liberty*, since if 'the object aimed at is good, if the compulsion employed such as to attain it, and if the good obtained overbalances the inconvenience of the compulsion itself, I do not understand how, upon utilitarian principles, the compulsion can be bad'. Stephen also took issue with Mill's support for the Religion of Humanity. Though he too upheld an ideal of intellectual aristocracy, Thomas Carlyle rejected Mill's plea for liberty vehemently, adding, to his brother, 'as if it were a sin to control, or coerce into better methods, human swine in any way'.

Other critics have also detected sinister aims in *On Liberty*. An early biographer of Mill, W. L. Courtney, asserted in 1889 that his 'object is...to replace what is ordinarily termed Religion by the Positivist conception of a religion of Humanity'. Writing in 1963, the historian Maurice Cowling, too, thought that '*On Liberty*, contrary to common opinion, was not so much a plea for individual freedom, as a means of ensuring that Christianity would be superseded by that form of liberal, rationalistic utilitarianism which went by the name of the Religion of Humanity', which to a humanist, of course, is not sinister at all. Another historian, Stefan Collini, also notes the 'extent to which Mill's moral ideal involved an extraordinarily close coincidence of *feelings* among all members of the human race', which resulted in 'an unnervingly intense yearning for total harmony' evident in *Utilitarianism* in particular. Thus, says Collini, 'The celebration of "enlarged altruism", and the corresponding presumption that conflict must represent the expression of selfishness...is hardly the voice of the textbook stereotype of liberal individualism.'

Chapter 5
Later writings, 1861–79

Utilitarianism (1861)

On Liberty's defence of freedom was based on 'utility in the largest sense, grounded on the permanent interests of man as a progressive being'. *Utilitarianism* aims to show how promoting greater individuality is compatible with pursuing the greatest happiness for all. Its overarching goal is to defend a secular ethics against theologically based morality for a broadly traditionalist general public. Mill's starting point is that 'Utility, or the Greatest Happiness Principle', holds that actions are 'right in proportion as they tend to promote happiness, wrong as they tend to produce the reverse of happiness'. We judge the rectitude of acts by their consequences; hence the theory is termed consequentialist. The 'utilitarian standard of what is right in conduct, is not the agent's own happiness, but that of all concerned'. 'By happiness is intended pleasure, and the absence of pain; by unhappiness, pain, and the privation of pleasure.' The 'only things desirable as ends' are 'pleasure, and freedom from pain', and 'all desirable things … are desirable either for the pleasure inherent in themselves, or as means to the promotion of pleasure and the prevention of pain'. This would become one of the most influential positions in modern philosophy, and, though doubts in particular have been expressed as to whether pleasure is the sole intrinsic good, it is still widely considered as a classic statement of modern

humanism. As we have seen, however, Mill's essay on 'Bentham' had already modified how he understood utility, for both pleasure and pain must be conceived collectively, so that sacrifices resulting from a desire for virtue are pleasurable even when they also involve pain to us.

Higher and lower pleasures

But what precisely is happiness? From Bain onwards, commentators have faulted Mill for not defining it carefully enough. Following Helvétius, who reduced all pleasure to sensual stimulation, and thought justice consisted in 'performing action useful to the greatest number', Bentham had focused on measuring enjoyable stimuli quantitatively, by criteria like intensity, duration, certainty, and propinquity, or distance from us. Mill denies that 'the estimation of pleasures should be supposed to depend on quantity alone', and aims at ranking them, as Hartley had done. This is usually regarded as his major contribution to utilitarianism. Against 'pig-philosophy' accusations, Mill insists, implying the need to consider self-development, that 'some kinds of pleasure are more desirable and more valuable than others'. Experience, not intuition, teaches us that the 'superiority of mental over bodily pleasures' lay 'chiefly in the greater permanency, safety, uncostliness, &c., of the former'. Mill wrote in his short-lived but revealing diary in 1854 that 'Quality as well as quantity of happiness is to be considered; less of a higher kind is preferable to more of a lower.' In the phrase always associated with the essay, *Utilitarianism* argued that 'It is better to be a human being dissatisfied than a pig satisfied; better to be Socrates dissatisfied than a fool satisfied.' (We recall that Socrates suffered the death penalty for defying Athens' rulers, as well as the fact that intellectuals are often more unhappy than others because the world is so irrational.) Swinishness and individuality have no relation to one another: we cannot become refined and discerning devotees to the lower pleasures, wallowing in decadence. A 'sense of dignity' induces us to prefer 'the pleasures of the intellect, of the

feelings and imagination, and of the moral sentiments', giving them 'a much higher value as pleasures than to those of mere sensation'. But is this 'sense' innate, of the 'moral sense' type Bentham dismissed, or acquired, like the high-mindedness and nobility of character commended by Aristotle?

Mill tells us that, 'Of two pleasures, if there be one to which all or almost all who have experience of both give a decided preference, irrespective of any feeling of moral obligation to prefer it, that is the more desirable pleasure.' Those 'who are equally acquainted with, and equally capable of appreciating and enjoying, both, do give a most marked preference to the manner of existence which employs their higher faculties'. So much for the stereotypically decadent artist or poet; and Socrates, it seems, must have had some swinish moments. To keep our 'sense of dignity' or 'nobler feelings' uppermost, utilitarianism 'could only attain its end by the general cultivation of nobleness of character'. So 'dignity' seems mostly acquired. Mill meant by this that rather than being merely 'selfish and base' we have 'feeling and conscience', and only reluctantly sink into 'a lower grade of existence'. He admitted that 'it may possibly be doubted whether a noble character is always the happier for its nobleness'—his own unhappiness surely proved that. But there was 'no doubt that it makes other people happier, and that the world in general is immensely a gainer by it'. Selfishness, and inadequate mental cultivation, are the chief causes of an unsatisfactory life.

Critics have raised various objections to these arguments. Is Mill a 'hedonist' at all? Is he an 'act' or a 'rule' utilitarian? When calculating the consequences of our actions is too difficult, how important are secondary principles like keeping promises or telling the truth? Do we really only desire pleasure? Why should our own happiness, or that of our family or group, not be preferable to that of everyone or anyone else? Must we always desire the greatest happiness, or can we settle for not harming others? What happens when my happiness results in your

unhappiness, or that of the 51 per cent makes the 49 per cent unhappy? What happens when desires for various forms of pleasure conflict with each other? How do we know when to defer to other people's judgments, when they claim to have experience we lack? Does, as the philosopher F. H. Bradley thought, preferring higher to lower pleasures imply abandoning the central utilitarian goal of a quantitative increase in happiness for the majority? Does it mean we may often be 'wrong' in our choice of pleasures? And doesn't this automatically create a two-tier system of pleasure judgment? One utilitarian today, Richard Layard, complains that what Mill 'should have said is that there are different causes of happiness—those that produce enduring effects on happiness and those whose effects are transient'. To Alan Ryan, these debates are clearly bound up with Mill's discussion of the 'Art of Life' in the *Logic* and elsewhere, where 'art' is related to the 'imperative mood' and is chiefly concerned with rules rather than truths. As a branch of art, ethics helps define the end aimed at, an end which includes progressively improving both the individual and society.

Much of this debate has focused on the qualitative/quantitative distinction. This too presents many problems. Not only might we derive equal pleasure from push-pin or poetry, depending on our mood. Even notionally 'lower' pleasures are not 'merely' sensual. Take the example of eating. This seems obviously to be a lower or bodily pleasure. We may appease the pangs of hunger by tipping a tin of cold baked beans onto a slice of white bread. Or we may indulge in a five-course meal at a fine French restaurant, replete with wine matching every course, and demanding an extensive knowledge of food and drink, allowing every savoured bite to enrich the flow of conversation, and defining the experience as a social occasion by communing with family and friends. In this case eating is clearly *also* a higher pleasure, and one moreover embedded in sociability. The same might be inferred of other supposedly lower or 'animal' pleasures. Can we really rank them, as opposed to saying that they give us different forms of pleasure

according to our mood and needs at any one time? Surely it is the balance of pleasures, our character, and 'harm' which need to be prioritized.

Therefore, is it not the act itself but our approach to it, the refinement of our sensibilities, our interactions with others, and the depth of our pockets, which defines the higher/lower difference? This makes our perception of what pleasure is much more complicated. Epicurean moderation in all things is a general rule here. Push-pin is less demanding than reading poetry, but the latter refines our sensibilities to a much greater degree. Overindulgence of any one desire is no good: Mill writes of our need for 'many and various pleasures'. We remember, too, that the essay on Bentham faulted the master for having an overly narrow conception of human nature. The same charge applies here. At the end of the day, Mill was no more representative of humanity than Bentham; to the Comtist Frederic Harrison he was 'a man to whom the ordinary amusements, humours, and passions of life were as utterly unknown as were its follies and its vices'. His inferences about the 'lower' pleasures must be taken *cum grano salis*.

Then there is the problem of virtue, whose worth, against the 'pig-philosophy' charge, Mill was greatly concerned to defend. Utilitarianism 'enjoins and requires the cultivation of the love of virtue up to the greatest strength possible, as being above all things important to the general happiness'. The general happiness is 'a good to the aggregate of all persons'. The 'highest virtue which can be found in man' is the willingness to sacrifice our own happiness for that of others. But why should we do so? Mill's 'proof' here is that 'the sole evidence it is possible to produce that anything is desirable, is that people do actually desire it', such that 'No reason can be given why the general happiness is desirable, except that each person, so far as he believes it to be attainable, desires his own happiness.' This has provoked the widespread objection that things are *not* 'desirable' normatively, in the sense of 'ought to be desired', simply because people *do* desire them

empirically. We want many things which are not good for us, or other people, or conducive to our happiness, or theirs. It is much harder to 'prove' why we should sacrifice our own happiness to promote general well-being than it is that we desire our own happiness. But society must persuade us to make the sacrifice. To Mill, 'education and opinion, which have so vast a power over human character, should so use that power as to establish in the mind of every individual an indissoluble association between his own happiness and the good of the whole'. This followed 'from the conception of our own happiness as a unit, neither more nor less valuable than that of another, or, in Christian language, the doctrine of loving one's neighbour as oneself'. 'In the golden rule of Jesus of Nazareth', Mill thus suggested, 'we read the complete spirit of the ethics of utility.' 'All honour', then, 'to those who can abnegate for themselves the personal enjoyment of life, when by such renunciation they contribute worthily to increase the amount of happiness in the world.'

Dignity seemingly plays little role in motivating us to be virtuous. We do take pleasure in gratifying and helping others, even if it involves a short-term sacrifice on our part, or more. Virtue offers its own reward. We may fear divine retribution, but Mill thought this a groundless sanction not worth encouraging. Social pressure is vastly more important. In 'Remarks on Bentham's Philosophy' (1833), Mill insisted that 'feeling' or 'conscience' made up a 'social interest' which drove us towards virtue. We hope for the favour of others by a show of good will. In evading our duty, we may feel the pangs of conscience, rooted in 'the social feelings of mankind, the desire to be in unity with our fellow creatures', which sounds like a (socially constructed) moral sense theory. Mill thought these would strengthen with 'an improving state of the human mind' as divisive superstitions declined—an interesting counterbalance to egotistical 'miserable individuality'. He also asserts that 'The ultimate sanction...of all morality (external motives apart) [is] a subjective feeling in our own minds.' This too sounds like 'conscience' or internalized social mores.

In the final section, Mill attempts to ground justice and rights in utility, and argues that 'social utility' alone can arbitrate between conflicting standards of justice in deciding what measures are expedient or for the good of society. So 'general utility' is still the primary standard of justice.

Considerations on Representative Government (1863)

The third phase of Mill's self-described intellectual development, we recall, was one in which 'We were now much less democrats than I had been', because 'we dreaded the ignorance and especially the selfishness and brutality of the mass.' Like Tocqueville, Mill thought mass democracy was inevitable, but felt the franchise could only be exercised responsibly by reasonably educated people. The *Considerations* proposed to assist this process. Identifying and promoting the general interest in a system where 'sinister', sectional, or class interests were commonly dominant required both disinterested governors and a public-minded electorate, both ever in scarce supply. If the masses were 'duly sensible of the value of superior wisdom', however, they could follow the 'independent judgment of a specially instructed few', provided the latter remained 'responsible to the many'. So how could this new deference to and sense of duty from the educated be introduced?

The *Considerations* aims to reconcile the two main social principles, variously understood by Mill as Permanence and Progression, or Order and Progress, in terms of the 'types of human character' societies generated. Progress implied both 'the idea of moving onward' and 'quite as much the prevention of falling back', or stationariness. It required qualities of 'mental activity, enterprise, and courage'. We are again on the terrain of the free will debate, and engaged with the self-formation of character, described in *On Liberty* as individuality. A key issue was 'which of two common types of character, for the general good of humanity, it is most desirable should predominate—the active, or

the passive type; that which struggles against evils, or that which endures them; that which bends to circumstances, or that which endeavours to make circumstances bend to itself'. The passive type of character, thought Mill, offering another ethological generalization, 'is favoured by the government of one or a few, and the active self-helping type by that of the Many'.

While the *Considerations* defends representative institutions as 'the ideally best form of government', Mill is here politically at his most conservative and relativist. Such institutions do not suit all peoples in all times. Even at their best they exhibit demonstrable weaknesses, and pose two key problems: 'a low grade of intelligence in the representative body, and in the popular opinion which controls it', and the 'danger of class legislation on the part of the numerical majority, these being all composed of the same class'. That adult (male) suffrage should be universal was the acme of radicalism. Without relinquishing his long-term commitment to popular sovereignty, Mill now set out a scheme for giving greater weight to minorities and the educated. He abandoned his support for the secret ballot, and rejected Chartist pleas for paying MPs. He supported an elected second chamber, not one composed of hereditary peers. But his most important proposals concern representing minorities.

Representing minorities and limiting the franchise

One way of avoiding majoritarian tyranny was proportional representation. First-past-the-post systems rewarded the slenderest majority in any constituency, effectively disfranchising the rest. A much fairer system would make every vote count. In early 1859, Mill discovered a scheme designed by the lawyer Thomas Hare, which proposed transferring votes to other candidates from the same party once a certain minimum had been reached to elect someone, thus ensuring a much more accurate representation of voters' intentions. Now widely adopted, this is called the single transferable vote system. Another way to hinder

majoritarianism was to limit or qualify voting rights. Mill had suggested excluding 'all who cannot read, write, and cipher' in 1835. The *Considerations* proposed a literacy and numeracy test (Bentham had supported the former), perhaps including some history, politics, and geography; plural voting for more educated electors; and (now against Bentham) banning all who had received poor relief in the past five years.

In total these measures might have eliminated half of the potential electorate at the time, though Mill also sought female enfranchisement. Mill remained a democrat, albeit of a type difficult to categorize. The scheme is only obliquely aimed at satisfying the utilitarian 'greatest happiness' criterion, still less the Benthamite injunction, 'everybody to count for one, nobody for more than one'. Promoting and protecting individuality has priority. It also smacks of paternalism, and reflects Mill's 1839 goal of government by means of the middle on behalf of the working classes. Many would be stuck in a vicious circle. Without the franchise to protect themselves, or prosperity sufficient to not require poor relief, what means did the workers have to avoid disdainful governments which did not adequately educate or help employ them to be able to vote?

This underscores for Mill both the distance between democracy and socialism, and for that matter democracy and liberalism, and his insistence that any democratic scheme had to rely on universal education. He had written in 1836 that 'High wages and universal reading are the two elements of democracy; where they co-exist, all government, except the government of public opinion, is impossible.' Anything less would impede the progress of rational argument. Ignorance was the mother of all tyranny. But there remained the problem of the supposedly more responsible educated minority. Mill recognized that merely being educated did not make people more public-minded. Nearly 'all the recognized professions have as such', he thought, 'interests & partialities opposed to the public good, & the members of Parliament whom

they would elect if organized apart would, I apprehend, be much more likely to represent their sentiments & objects as professional, than as educated men'. This weakened his capacity for faith in the intelligentsia as a class. He also worried that he had 'not seen any method proposed by which persons of educated minds can be sifted from the rest of the community'. Yet we also recognize here the reasonable assumption that more educated people tend to be more liberal, for they have been exposed to greater variety of opinion and practice. 'Stupid people', Mill famously remarked, were more likely to belong to the 'stupid party', the Conservatives. In his later approach to democracy, then, Mill was close to other liberal critics of a wide franchise, like the free trader John Bright, as well as various more conservative writers, including Henry Maine, Walter Bagehot, and W. E. H. Lecky. But we should recall, too, that Radicals like Thomas Paine had warned of 'the despotism of numbers'.

Two other issues raised in the *Considerations* generally interest modern readers: Mill's approach to nationalism, and his view of colonial and imperial government. Mill conceded that 'nationality', the union by common sympathies of a people based on language, history, and other factors, offered a powerful case for self-government, citing the Hungarian and Italian independence movements. He did not think that those seeking independence could necessarily expect assistance from others, though this would be justified if despotic powers like Russia suppressed them, as it did the Hungarians in 1849. Narrow, chauvinistic nationalism, however, he always rejected, preferring that 'the love of that larger country, the world, may be nursed into similar strength, both as a source of elevated emotion and as a principle of duty'. Later he supported the idea of 'a general Federation, or United States of Europe' as 'the ultimate result of human improvement'. Like Bentham, Mill thought settler colonies should generally become independent as soon as possible. But he did not oppose colonization as a means of alleviating population growth, and supported assisted schemes, especially respecting Australia, from the 1830s.

The problem of empire

Where Britain's empire was concerned, the independence of peoples was a different matter. Here Mill uncritically followed his father, who called 'English government in India with all its vices' 'a blessing of unspeakable magnitude to the population of Hindustan', who had only 'just emerged from barbarism'. (In fact, the Mohenjo-daro civilization was flourishing in the Indus valley *c.*2500 BCE.) James Mill felt that with 'a simple form of arbitrary government, tempered by European honour and European intelligence' 'even the utmost abuse of European power is better...than the most temperate exercise of Oriental despotism'. His son wrote in 1831 that it was 'part of the inevitable lot of mankind, that when they themselves are in a backward state of civilization, they are unsusceptible of being well governed'. This justified a 'vigorous despotism' until conquered territories reached a 'higher stage of improvement'—an extremely open-ended principle. In 1840, Mill was lecturing friends like Caroline Fox about British India and the 'advantages derived by its princes from our supremacy there'.

To the historian Eric Stokes, 'It was India which most clearly exposed the paradox in utilitarianism between the principle of liberty and the principle of authority'. Following the 1857 'Mutiny', the East India Company was abolished and its territories given over to direct rule from Westminster, a development Mill viewed with alarm. As a Company employee Mill did not implement utilitarian ideas as forcefully as his father. But readers today tend to view his position on British rule as self-serving, and a whitewashing of the brutal history of India's conquest. As he left the East India Company, Mill actually described British government in India as 'one of the purest in intention but one of the most beneficent in act, ever known among mankind'. Was he aware of the degree of greed and brutality involved in Britain's—and especially the East India Company's—conquest of India? Was he

acquainted with the severe famines, for example in 1770, which had accompanied the extreme exploitation of its people? (His father's *History of British India* nowhere belabours the point.) Did he know of Britain's destruction of India's textile industry—the world's largest in the 18th century—in order to sell Lancashire cloth under the guise of 'free trade'? Or did he view this as 'progress'?

The apparent duplicity of trumpeting liberty for (middle-class) whites and despotism for non-whites sullies Mill's reputation at this vital point. Modern readers have little tolerance for Mill's bald defence of empire. *On Liberty* had excused Britain's forcing of opium on China through two wars, 1839–42 and 1856–60, on the grounds of free trade principles, though widespread addiction resulted. It also said the Chinese had 'become stationary—have remained so for thousands of years; and if they are ever to be farther improved, it must be by foreigners'. The *Considerations* reiterated that in dependencies not in 'a sufficiently advanced state' 'a vigorous despotism is in itself the best mode of government for training the people in what is specifically wanting to render them capable of a higher civilization'. The degrading effects of such despotisms on both ruler and ruled seem not to have worried him greatly.

Mill did, admittedly, express regret on hearing of 'the atrocities perpetrated in the Indian Mutiny, and the feelings which supported them at home', as he did a few years later with 'the sympathy with the lawless rebellion of the Southern Americans in defence of an institution which is the sum of all lawlessness'. But his logic often seems self-serving. His 1854 diary noted:

> Perhaps the English are the fittest people to rule over barbarous or semi-barbarous nations like those of the East, precisely because they are the stiffest, and most wedded to their own customs, of all civilised people. All former conquerors of the East have been absorbed into it, and have adopted its ways, instead of

communicating to it their own. So did the Portuguese; so would the French have done. Not so John Bull; if he has one foot in India he will always have another on the English shore.

Of the East India Company he acknowledged, if only privately, the 'injustice & crime of many kinds by which their Indian empire was acquired'. Yet he supported virtually all the annexations of Indian states which took place during his employment with 'John Company', arguing that in many 'the military chiefs & office holders who carry on the government & form the ruling class are almost as much foreigners to the mass of the people as we ourselves are'. In Parliament in 1867 he declined to speak on the Orissa debate, respecting a famine in which a third of the population, some 4–5 million people, died, while 200 million pounds of rice were exported to Britain. (He was in fact attacked in the House of Commons as a source of the idea that the market would rectify supply and demand in such circumstances.) Mill knew that many Radicals, like Place, supported Indian independence. He knew of Bentham's opposition to colonies, and probably also his insistence on the superiority of Britons to Indians. He was also presumably aware of the substantial British positivist critique of imperialism; he knew Frederic Harrison well enough. But he seems nowhere to have taken it seriously, though he noted in 1868 that the 'advanced Comtist sect' in Britain 'do not at all go along with me'.

Indisputably, Mill's Indian experience led him both to counsel state-driven paternalism to solve the Irish 'problem', and to argue that landed property there might be used by the state as circumstances dictated, following custom in India, where the state was a universal landlord. But was Mill a racist? On occasion he used the language of race in a manner, aiming at ethological generalization, which would today be deemed racist. He told D'Eichthal in 1837 that 'I quite agree with you that an infusion of the Oriental character into that of the nations of northern Europe would form a combination very much better than either

separately'. In 1839, too, he wrote of 'the black race as compared with the European' of 'their love of repose & in the superior capacity of animal enjoyment & consequently of sympathetic sensibility, which is characteristic of the negro race', while adding 'that if our intelligence is more developed & our activity more intense, *they* possess exactly what is most needful to us as a qualifying counterpoise'.

But this indicates that Mill's discussion focused on character types: his beliefs in environmental influence were too strong for him to rely on ontological or innate categories of 'race'. Thus in 1865 he wrote to the Scottish lawyer John Boyd Kinnear that 'I think you ascribe too great influence to differences of race & too little to historical differences & to accidents as causes of the diversities of character & usage existing among mankind'. Elsewhere he stressed that 'education, legislation, and social circumstances' were 'of prodigiously greater efficacy than either race or climate or the two combined'. He was particularly critical of the French historian Jules Michelet for having 'carried the influence of Race too far', and noted that 'the earliest known civilization was, we have the strongest reason to believe, a negro civilization. The original Egyptians are inferred, from the evidence of their sculptures, to have been a negro race: it was from negroes, therefore, that the Greeks learned their first lessons in civilization'. For someone so enamoured of classical Greece this was a dramatic acknowledgement, though of possible Indian influence on Plato he was evidently silent. And Mill later stressed that

> I have long felt that the prevailing tendency to regard all the marked distinctions of human character as innate, and in the main indelible, and to ignore the irresistible proofs that by far the greater part of those differences, whether between individuals, races, or sexes, are such as not only might but naturally would be produced by differences in circumstances, is one of the chief hindrances to the rational treatment of great social questions, and one of the greatest stumbling blocks to human improvement. (I. 270)

We should also remember that Mill vehemently opposed slavery. He greatly lamented British support for the South during the American Civil War, and heartily championed abolitionism. He clashed with Carlyle over West Indian conditions, and chaired the Jamaica Committee, supported by Darwin, John Bright, Herbert Spencer, and the scientist T. H. Huxley, in an ultimately fruitless effort to prosecute the governor of Jamaica, Edward John Eyre, who brutally quashed a rebellion there in 1865. This became a *cause célèbre*, with Carlyle, John Ruskin, and Charles Dickens, among others, defending Eyre.

Nonetheless, Mill was emphatically a 'civilizationist', in the sense of believing that a higher economic efficiency, the rule of law, the prevalence of 'active' character types, and having representative institutions bestowed rights of rule over the less advanced. When the East India Company was dissolved, Mill summarized what he saw as the many advantages it had brought to India, including the suppression of Thuggee criminals, piracy, infanticide, Suttee, witchcraft, and slavery. He also, perhaps inadvertently, revealed how hugely profitable Company rule was. Citing the example of the widening and deepening of the Begaree Canal in Upper Sind, at a cost of £13,000, he noted that the expected return was £11,900 per annum.

Feminism and *The Subjection of Women* (1869)

As an extension of democracy and natural rights theories, feminism had been one logical implication of radicalism from the 1790s onwards. But many male reformers ignored the connection. Written with Harriet in 1861, *The Subjection of Women* represented the culmination of Mill's rejection of his father's opposition to female suffrage in the 1820s, which had been greatly reinforced by Harriet's influence. Modern feminists often find the text somewhat staid and tame. Mill was even evasive about the question of divorce, and, wanting to know much more about what women thought about it, refused to commit himself publicly on

the issue. (Privately he favoured a simple dissolution by either party.) It did not fare well at first, and was the only book of Mill's which lost his publisher money. But the *Subjection* became the foremost feminist tract of the age, and 'aroused the most antagonism', Michael Packe thought, of 'anything Mill ever wrote'.

The *Subjection*'s central argument is that the legal and moral subjection of women was 'the latest remaining relic of the primitive condition of society, the tyranny of physical force', prior to the substitution, 'as the general principle of human relations', of 'a just equality, instead of the dominion of the strongest'. Equality is seen as a corollary of liberty, and a goal of progress generally. Here a republican rejection of domination as such comes to the fore, as does Mill's opposition to religiously based ethics. (An 1848 letter to G. J. Holyoake described current ideas of women and the family as 'founded on and connected with' 'the whole priestly morality…which morality, in my opinion, thorough[ly] deserves the epithets of "intolerant, slavish, and selfish"'.) The *Subjection* also meshed with Mill's neo-Malthusianism, and the idea that no alteration in 'the perpetuation of the previous degradation of women' could be expected 'while their whole lives are devoted to the function of producing and rearing children'. It summed up the discussions about marriage, divorce, and relations between the sexes which he and Harriet had commenced early in their relationship, when she had suggested that marriage might be superseded when both sexes were legally equal and women fully controlled their reproductive rights. Its principles were also outlined in a substantial number of co-authored newspaper articles and letters dealing with domestic violence and other marital issues.

The text consists of four chapters. The first outlines the general case against the legal subordination of women to men, which is described as both wrong in itself and a great obstacle to general improvement. The most common argument for such subordination, the naturally greater weakness of women, Mill

99

counts as unproven, since women have been barred from many positions where they might have achieved as much as men, if not more. Chapter 2 describes marriage as a condition of bonded servitude for women, who lack property rights, separate rights of inheritance, rights over their children, and usually the right of divorce. Chapter 3 returns to the claim that women should be excluded from specific professions, and contends that only free, meritocratic competition can establish any justifiable limits. Chapter 4 then summarizes the general benefits of gender equality, which include providing a much more just model of human relations, substantially increasing the volume of intelligence available to foster social progress, and, most important of all, securing greater happiness for half of humanity.

Mill's feminism also extended to his defence of women against state inspection for venereal disease during the controversy over the Contagious Diseases Act in 1870–1. Here, responding to a parliamentary committee, Mill, while not opposed to underage girls engaged in prostitution being forcibly removed to 'some industrial home', objected to inspections of prostitutes, and thought it no 'part of the business of the Government to provide securities beforehand against the consequences of immoralities of any kind'. Asked whether brothel-keepers should be prosecuted, he was unable to offer an opinion.

Mill thus treated female equality as part of a general argument favouring utilitarianism. He felt that women tended to improve the moral tenor of public life, writing elsewhere that 'the common voice of mankind proclaims them superior in moral goodness'. He also thought them likelier than men to protect areas of natural beauty, so that 'Women's suffrage will help us in this as in so many other things, for women will be much more unwilling than men to submit to the expulsion of all beauty from common life.' Mill's renewed assertion of feminism reinforced his ideas of equality. The *Subjection* spoke of 'that practical feeling of the equality of human beings, which is the theory of Christianity, but which

Christianity will never practically teach, while it sanctions institutions grounded on an arbitrary preference of one human being over another'. Now he insisted that 'command and obedience are but unfortunate necessities of human life: society in equality is its normal state. Already in modern life, and more and more as it progressively improves, command and obedience become exceptional facts in life, equal association its general rule.' He added that 'the true virtue of human beings is fitness to live together as equals; claiming nothing for themselves but what they as freely concede to every one else; regarding command of any kind as an exceptional necessity, and in all cases a temporary one'.

Socialism and the land question

In his later years, with Harriet long dead, Mill again addressed socialism. Some believe his criticisms in the unfinished 'Chapters on Socialism' (1879), begun in 1869, indicate the decay of her influence. Mill clearly rejected Marx's revolutionary socialism. (He did however comment on an anti-war speech by Marx to the International Workingmen's Association in 1870 that he was 'highly pleased with the address. There was not one word in it that ought not to be there.') He still condemned as 'a failure of the social arrangements' a system where the 'reward, instead of being proportioned to the labour and abstinence of the individual, is almost in an inverse ratio to it: those who receive the least, labour and abstain the most'. He lamented that 'The very idea of distributive justice, or any proportionality between success and merit, or between success and exertion, is, in the present state of society, so manifestly chimerical as to be relegated to the region of romance.' Mill upheld his lifelong support for competition as the most efficient incentive to production. But he did not retreat from his wider sympathy for socialist ends, and insisted that small-scale communities of the Owenite or Fourierist type, 'a world governed by public spirit', were still eminently practicable, even if the 'attempt to manage the whole production of a nation by one central organization is a totally different matter'. Even these communities,

however, he thought 'at present workable only by the *élite* of mankind'. (In *The Subjection of Women* Mill had stressed that, 'For my own part, I am one of the strongest supporters of community of goods, when resulting from an entire unity of feeling in the owners, which makes all things common between them.')

The land question concerned Mill frequently in later years. Coleridge, the Saint-Simonians, and his Indian experience had taught him that approaches to property varied enormously across the ages, and that no absolute right to the land existed, property rights being, in Alan Ryan's phrasing, a social privilege rather than a corollary from the liberty principle. Though he favoured 'common ownership in the raw material of the globe', he rejected immediate nationalization on the grounds of the size of the indemnity required, but argued that 'Lands not yet appropriated by individuals should, I think, by no means be allowed to pass into private ownership but should be sacred to public purposes.' In 1868 he founded the Land Tenure Reform Association, which promoted the state purchase of land for co-operative farms, the prohibition of further privatization of public land, state management of lands belonging to public institutions and endowed bodies, and 'keeping open extensive tracts in a state of wild natural beauty and freedom'. This entailed a larger sphere of state activity than Mill had hitherto proposed. The association also urged taxation on the 'unearned' increase in land values, and enlisted the support of Alfred Russel Wallace, the co-discoverer of the theory of evolution, who later formed the Land Nationalisation Society, which Helen Taylor supported. (She later joined H. M. Hyndman's Democratic Federation, which advocated socialism.) But Mill did not concede that a similar principle of taxation should be extended to, for example, the increasing value of railway shares or works of art, describing this as 'the earnings and recompense of human labour and thrift'.

In 1865, Mill was elected a Liberal Member of Parliament for Westminster. His career as an MP lasted only three years. He was

8. John Stuart Mill (1806–73).

not a powerful public speaker and was too earnest for the men's club atmosphere of the House. He supported introducing death duties on landed estates, and abolishing flogging except for crimes of violence, though he shocked John Bright and others by defending the death penalty for murder as the 'least cruel mode' of deterring crime. (But he opposed cruelty to animals.) Most notably, in 1867 he introduced the first bill proposing suffrage for

women. His role in prosecuting Eyre was a major reason for his defeat, along with his support for the atheist Charles Bradlaugh, who had been elected an MP but was then excluded for his beliefs. Mill's enemies attempted to discredit him by quoting him referring to the working classes as 'generally liars', but found that when he admitted this in public he was met with 'vehement applause' for his honesty (see Figure 8).

Three Essays on Religion (1874)

We have seen that Mill's defence of liberty and his wish to avoid fatalism were closely linked to his attitudes towards religion. His opposition to Christianity and wish to replace it with utilitarianism runs as a guiding thread throughout his thought from youth to old age. The historian Joseph Hamburger describes the 'elimination of Christianity' as 'a matter of policy' for Mill. Already in 1823 he signed a letter addressed to the 'infidel' Richard Carlile, 'An Atheist'. Mill wrote Comte that he had 'had the rather rare fate in my country of never having believed in God, even as a child, I always saw in the creation of a true social philosophy the only possible base for the general regeneration of human morality, and in the idea of Humanity the only one capable of replacing that of God'. Harriet's atheism doubtless helped push him towards secularism. But he was exceptionally cautious as to how this was to be achieved. In 1834, he informed Carlyle that 'the existence of a Creator is not to me a matter of faith or of intuition...it is but a hypothesis, the proofs of which, as you I know agree with me, do not amount to absolute certainty'. The same was true of 'the immortality of the soul'. There was 'no reason to believe that it perishes; nor sufficient ground for complete assurance that it survives'. Hence, 'all appearances and probabilities are in favour of the cessation of our consciousness when our earthly mechanism ceases to work'.

Like his father and Bentham, Mill considered religious belief to corrode both morality and epistemology. The *Logic* stated that 'the

order of human progression in all respects will be a corollary deducible from the order of progression in the intellectual convictions of mankind, that is, from the law of the successive transformations of religion and science'. Mill might have written 'from religion towards science'. For here he was wholly with Comte: religion was the greatest barrier to human progress, conceived as the triumph of scientific understanding. In 1854, he noted privately 'the grossly immoral pattern of morality' which humanity had 'always set up for themselves in the person of their Gods, whether of revelation or of nature'. Mill was, he wrote in 1861, 'an enemy to no religions but those which appear to me to be injurious either to the reasoning powers or the moral sentiments', but this included all which claimed a god who was omnipotent, 'for such persons are obliged to maintain that evil is good'. ('Belief of a cruel god makes a cruel man', wrote Thomas Paine, whom we can be reasonably sure Mill had read—Carlile had been imprisoned for printing his theological works.) The *Logic* championed what Mill called 'disbelief', where not only grounds for doubting a claim are present, but the belief defies our sense of scientific laws. Thus, Mill wrote in 1863, 'there is not a single miracle in either the Old or New Testament the particular evidence of which is worth a farthing. Those of Christ seem to me exactly on a level with the wonderful stories current about every remarkable man, & repeated in good faith in times when the scientific spirit scarcely existed.' Regarding God's existence, crucially, such claims were presented by 'many a deluded visionary' as intuitive, which were really 'a conclusion drawn from appearances to his senses or feelings in his internal consciousness which were altogether an insufficient foundation for any such belief'. And he refused to accept 'that the succession of historical events requires any supernatural explanation'.

Often underestimated by scholars, the centrality of Mill's engagement with religion needs underscoring. Against Alan Ryan's widely accepted portrayal of Mill as a secular figure, the political theorist Linda Raeder describes him as having had 'an

essentially religious nature in search of a god'. This can be challenged. Consider how Mill described the process of prayer in 1868, in terms of 'the effect produced on the mind of the person praying, not by the belief that it will be granted, but by the elevating influence of an endeavour to commune and to become in harmony with the highest spiritual ideal that he is capable in elevated moments of conceiving'. Here an idealized moral self, not 'god', was central to Mill. In 1861, he condoned those who had 'privately consecrated an internal altar to an *ideal* Perfect Being, to whose ideal will he endeavour to conform his own'. We also have Harriet's summary of the 'Three Essays' as aiming at

> throwing over all doctrines and theories, called religion, as devices for power, to show how religion & poetry fill the same want, the craving after higher objects, the consolation of suffering, by hopes of heaven for the selfish, love of God for the tender & grateful—how all this must be superseded by morality deriving its power from sympathies and benevolence and its reward from the approbation of those we respect.

This is humanism, not religion.

But Mill was extremely cautious about publicly expressing his scepticism. As his friend the working-class secularist G. J. Holyoake commented, 'No writer ever guarded his words and conduct more assiduously than J. S. Mill.' In 1845, he wrote Comte that 'Today, I believe, one ought to keep total silence on the question of religion when writing for an English audience, though indirectly one may strike any blow one wishes at religious beliefs.' In 1861, Mill explained

> that neither in the *Logic* nor in any other of my publications had I any purpose of undermining Theism; nor, I believe, have most readers of the *Logic* perceived any such tendency in it. I am far from thinking that it would be a benefit to mankind in general, if without any other change in them, they could be made disbelievers in all

religion; nor would I willingly weaken in any person the reverence for Christ, in which I myself very strongly participate. (XV. 754)

For practical purposes Mill was an atheist. But it was dangerous to admit this publicly, as Charles Bradlaugh and others learned to their great cost. As his friend Henry Reeve remarked, if his 'absolute rejection of the principles of religious faith and of the accountability of man to God' were known 'they would stand but little chance of obtaining a hearing on any other subject'. Hair-splitting and prevarication were required. In 1865 Mill insisted that refusing to 'worship no God but a good God is to be an atheist'. In 1868, he wrote a correspondent, 'If any one again tells you that I am an atheist, I would advise you to ask him, how he knows and in what page of my numerous writings he finds anything to bear out the assertion.' 'I am not anxious to bring over any but really superior intellects & characters to the whole of my own opinions', he told Bain in 1859, 'in the case of all others I would much rather, as things now are, try to improve their religion than to destroy it'. This argument favoured the utility of some types of religion for the masses, while still generally supporting rationalism. Praising 'the mind which cherishes devotion to a Principle of Good in the universe', Mill thought, 'I do not think it can ever be best for mankind to *believe* what there is not evidence of', but 'we sh[oul]d encourage ourselves to believe as to the unknowable what it is best for mankind that we sh[oul]d believe'. In 1871, he insisted that 'the cultivation of the idea of a perfectly good & wise being & of the desire to help the purposes of such a being is morally beneficial in the highest degree though the belief that this being is omnipotent & therefore the creator of physical & moral evil is as demoralizing a belief as can be entertained'. But how to separate the two? Nature could not be a model for describing any supreme being. For

Any one who considers the course of nature, without the usual predetermination to find all excellent, must see that it has been made, if made at all, by an extremely imperfect being; that it can be

accounted for on no theory of a just ruler, unless that ruler is of extremely limited power, and hemmed in by obstacles which he is unable to overcome.

Did Mill then become more 'religious' during the period that the posthumously published *Nature, The Utility of Religion*, and *Theism* (1874) were composed? (The first two were written between 1850 and 1858, the last between 1868 and 1870.) In 1861 he conceded that the view that 'the world was made, in whole or in part, by a powerful Being who cared for man, appears to me, though not proved, yet a very probable hypothesis', if one which 'must remain...uncertain'. This did not stop one theological journal from denouncing him as the 'chief of the Satanic School in England'. Some think Mill's deep grief after Harriet's death may explain an apparent accommodation. Certainly in later years Mill gave greater stress to the Christian basis of a future morality, writing in 1872 that 'I look upon it as the great work now to be done, to build up a system of morals capable of inspiring enthusiasm & satisfying the intellect. My own belief is that this will be a developement of Xtianity, properly understood.' The crucial achievement would be to extract what was morally useful from religion, and to discard what was harmful. Thus 'Honesty, self sacrifice, love of our fellow-creatures, & the desire to be of use in the world, constitute the true point of resemblance between those whose religion however overlaid with dogmas is genuine, & those who are genuinely religious without any dogmas at all.' So here 'genuinely religious' really means 'utilitarian'.

The three essays of 1874 have different aims. The first rejected the idea that any evidence existed of benevolent divine guidance of the world. Mill told Herbert Spencer: 'You look upon nature as something we should do well to follow', whereas 'I look upon nature as a horrible old harridan'. However Wordsworth rhapsodized about it, nature was cruel, and this meant God was too. Mill reasoned in 1850 that 'If the maker of the world *can* all that he will, then he wills misery'. The second essay defended the

utility of a Religion of Humanity, insisting that 'Belief…in the supernatural, great as are the services which it rendered in the early stages of human development, cannot be considered to be any longer required, either for enabling us to know what is right and wrong in social morality, or for supplying us with motives to do right and to abstain from wrong.' Instead, as Morley put it, 'the sense of unity with mankind, and a deep feeling for the general good, may be cultivated into a sentiment and a principle which would fulfil the functions of religion better than any form whatever of supernaturalism'. This followed Bentham's argument that 'religious obligation, when not enforced by public opinion, produces scarcely any effect on conduct'.

The third essay, written after Harriet's death, most surprised some of Mill's followers in its apparent concessions to arguments from design. Startlingly, Mill even posited vis-à-vis Darwin that 'the adaptations in Nature afford a large balance of probability in favour of creation by intelligence', even if this was 'no more than a probability'. John Morley, who caused a scandal by spelling God with a small 'g' in the *Fortnightly Review*, wrote that it 'dismayed his disciples not merely as an infelicitous compromise with orthodoxy, but, what was far more formidable, as actually involving a fatal relaxation of his own rules and methods of reasoning', particularly in 'Mill's modified acceptance of the argument from Design'. Himmelfarb too terms it a 'retreat from rationalism'. Late Victorian secularists like John M. Robertson found the idea of 'a good deity of limited powers'—a doctrine verging on Manichaean dualism—untenable. Mill also acknowledged the possibility of Christ's having undertaken a divine mission, though not as the son of God—also 'unwarrantable' to Robertson—and described him as 'one of the very few historical characters for whom I have a real and high respect'. But Mill also insisted that 'Even the Christ of the Gospels holds out the direct promise of reward from heaven as a primary inducement to the noble and beautiful beneficence towards our fellow-creatures which he so impressively inculcates. This is a

radical inferiority of the best supernatural religions, compared with the Religion of Humanity.'

It has been argued that 'This recognition of a finite God, on an interim basis, constituted [Mill's] chief amendment of the Comtean religion of humanity.' Morley deplored 'the virtual elevation of naked and arbitrary possibilities into the place of reasonable probabilities'. But did Mill go so far? He insists, with respect to God's existence, that 'there is evidence, but insufficient for proof, and amounting only to one of the lower degrees of probability', which seemingly conflicts with 'a large balance of probability'. This meant the 'whole domain of the supernatural is thus removed from the region of Belief into that of simple Hope'. Mill asserts that 'The notion of a providential government by an omnipotent Being for the good of his creatures must be entirely dismissed', and that belief in a benevolent creator 'is not only not justified by any evidence but is a conclusion in opposition to such evidence as we have'. He acknowledges only that 'such evidence as there is, points to the creation, not indeed of the universe, but of the present order of it by an Intelligent Mind, whose power over the materials was not absolute, whose love for his creatures was not his sole actuating inducement, but who nevertheless desired their good'. Among other things, this substantially undermined ideas of a naturally harmonious world with the 'market' being guided by a divine 'invisible hand' to the most beneficial ends for humanity. To Carlyle's view that slavery was divinely ordained, too, Mill countered that 'If "the gods"... will this, it is the first duty of human beings to resist such gods. Omnipotent those "gods" are not, for powers which demand human tyranny and injustice cannot accomplish their purpose unless human beings cooperate.' Arguments about a future life were 'none at all'; and in any case, 'History, so far as we know it, bears out the opinion, that mankind can perfectly well do without the belief in a heaven.'

So there was little sustenance here for orthodox believers. Instead, Mill insisted that 'The essence of religion is the strong and earnest

direction of the emotions and desires towards an ideal object, recognized as of the highest excellence, and as rightfully paramount over all selfish objects of desire.' This condition, he thought, was 'fulfilled by the Religion of Humanity in as eminent a degree, and in as high a sense, as by the supernatural religions even in their best manifestations, and far more so than in any of their others'.

Mill's reputation

The 'deepest of our living thinkers' (in the historian H. T. Buckle's words), Mill died in Avignon, France, on 7 May 1873, leaving half his estate to the cause of women's education. The *Subjection* long remained controversial, but Mill's feminism found support from Millicent Garrett Fawcett, her husband the Liberal MP Henry Fawcett, and many others. At his death Mill had, in Leslie Stephen's estimate, 'probably more followers than any other teacher' in the English universities. At the peak of his reputation, between 1860 and 1870, wrote Albert Venn Dicey in 1905, 'His authority among the educated youth of England was greater than may appear credible to the present generation. His work *On Liberty* was to the younger body of Liberal statesmen a political manual.' One account even termed it 'the gospel of the nineteenth century'. John Morley called him the 'foremost instructor of his time in wisdom and goodness', and a man who saw progress as possible 'only on condition of enlightened and strenuous effort on the part of persons of superior character and opportunity'. The *Principles* was generally regarded as a turning point in economic thinking. As late as 1900, Leslie Stephen wrote, 'In spite of many attacks, it still holds a position among standard textbooks.' 'It was well said of him', the Irish historian Justin McCarthy remarked, 'that he had reconciled political economy with humanity.' Walter Bagehot's obituary summed up Mill's achievement as

> the first among great English economists who has ventured to
> maintain that the present division of the industrial community into

labourers and capitalist is neither destined nor adapted for a long continued existence: that a large production of wealth is much less important than a good distribution of it: that a state of industry in which both capital and population are stationary is as favourable to national well-being as one in which they are advancing: that fixed customs are perpetually modifying the effects which unrestrained competition would of itself inevitably produce: that a large body of peasant proprietors is usually a source of great national advantage: and that a system of emigration on a great scale would be productive of much benefit to the English peasantry by raising their habitual standard of comfort, and therefore putting a check on the reckless increase of a miserable population.

By 1900, however, Millite liberalism was waning. 'It was', wrote Frederic Harrison, 'the dominant school of the "sixties": it is dominant no more.' Gradually Mill's texts were challenged; to William Stanley Jevons the *Logic* was a 'maze of self-contradictions'. Yet to Dicey, Mill came to be seen as *the* pivotal figure: 'The changes or fluctuations in Mill's own convictions, bearing as they do in many points upon legislative opinion, are at once the sign, and were in England, to a great extent, the cause, of the transition from the individualism of 1830–1865 to the collectivism of 1900.' Already in 1885, thought Henry Sidgwick, 'Individualism of the extreme kind has clearly had its day.' The late Victorians increasingly saw government as able to promote individual happiness. New Liberals in the 1890s and later, like Leonard Hobhouse, thought the state could assist self-development, which Hobhouse saw not in terms of pleasure but of capacities and energies. Another New Liberal, John Hobson, saw in Mill 'a larger measure of disinterestedness, a keener feeling for humanity, and more rigorous standards of intellectual honesty than other thinkers of his day', and praised 'his frank recognition of the failure of the "simple system of natural liberty" to produce any guarantee for a tolerable economic condition of society, [which] together with the abandonment of the central operative principle of capitalism, the wage–fund theory, heralded the

downfall of the science whose completion he had been recently celebrating'.

As socialism became more popular, Mill was increasingly seen as a progenitor. Hobson noted that '"Socialism" and the accompanying political disillusionment of [Mill's] later years were the inevitable product of the thought of a new age which had left philosophic radicalism a generation behind it.' The Liberal politician Charles Dilke said Mill, 'very far from being an individualist, was abreast of the most modern tendencies in a socialist direction, and, so far from being stationary in his opinions was moving in the van. Indeed he was perhaps the first English politician to inaugurate a movement dealing with the land question, which was socialistic in its aims.' A generation later the political theorist Ernest Barker wrote that 'Mill prepared above all others the way for the new development of English thought which appears after 1880 ... It is Mill who supplies the economic doctrine: it is Mill who serves, in the years between 1848 and 1880, as the bridge from laissez-faire to the idea of social readjustment by the State, and from political Radicalism to economic Socialism.' The Fabian Sidney Ball stated that, 'As regards my own position in relation to Socialism, I am content to be a follower of Mill, from whom I learned my first lessons in Socialism as well as in Liberalism.' But if Mill's influence generally waned around 1900, the Cold War saw a great revival of his reputation, when *On Liberty* came to be seen as championing liberalism's chief principle. Mill became a leading figure in the canon of 'great thinkers' once again.

Chapter 6
Mill today

The philosopher John Gray terms Mill '*the paradigm* liberal thinker'. But was he? If we take Mill at his word, his central achievement lay in being a paradigm-breaking visionary who refused to let the prejudices of his age obstruct humanity's progress towards a superior society. To Mill, the greatest problem in modern politics was maximizing *both* liberty and equality without endangering either unduly. We identify him today 'paradigmatically' with liberty. But he believed his emphasis on equality, encompassing feminism, socialism, and co-operation, most distinguished him from other liberals. Equality was fundamental to well-being, and a corollary of liberty: for most, there is no liberty in conditions of substantial inequality. Those who view Mill as unoriginal fail to appreciate that his combination of liberty and equality was a unique and compelling achievement in this period, and often also subsequently.

Reading Mill contextually and historically reveals that his ideas were constantly evolving. As a result, unsurprisingly, he is often accused of inconsistency or eclecticism. There are many variations on the 'two Mills' theme, with Harriet as his alter ego, or Comte, or James Mill, or merely 'earlier' and 'later'. (Isaiah Berlin writes of Mill's 'last, humanitarian-Socialist phase'.) Mill's opinions altered about socialism; about the secret ballot, which he initially supported but rejected in the *Considerations*; and about the risks

of majoritarian democracy, which strengthened his defence of individuality. He became less of a democrat and more of a socialist. He remained consistently a feminist and a neo-Malthusian. Late in life, in 1869, he thought that 'The emancipation of women and co-operative production' were 'the two great changes that will regenerate society'.

Certain themes recur in Mill's thought from the early 1830s: the need for open debate and clear thinking to discern the truth; opposition to intuitionism and established religion as obstacles to logical thinking; the irreconcilability of images of arbitrary or unjust gods with morality; support for the idea of free will as choosing one's own course in life, and as involving self-mastery and a rejection of fatalism; the value of individuality in defining this course; the need to minimize social interference in each person's life to foment this individuality; a commitment to equality, particularly of women, as a component in the 'greatest happiness'; the sole adequacy of representative political institutions and co-operative economic organization to attain these goals; the ideal of civilization as summarizing these achievements.

So did Mill have a 'system', and if so is it consistent? His disciple John Morley regarded the idea of perfectibility, inherited from Turgot and Condorcet, as linking *On Liberty*, *Utilitarianism*, and the speculative parts of the *Principles*, and thought Mill's 'devotion to the substantial good of the majority...binds together all the parts of his work, from the *System of Logic* down to his last speech on the Land Question'. Tensions pervade Mill's thought. The problem, however, is not that Mill supported multiple principles but arbitrating between them when they conflict, notably in *On Liberty*.

First and foremost was the idea of progress. To Alan Ryan, 'Mill's concern with self-development and moral progress is a strand in his philosophy to which almost everything else is subordinate'.

In 1826, Mill asserted that 'The most important quality of the human intellect is its progressiveness, its tendency to improvement.' Progress was from the barbaric to the civilized, defined in 1836 as 'human beings acting together for common purposes in large bodies, and enjoying the pleasures of social intercourse'. A 'state of high civilization' required 'the diffusion of property and intelligence, and the power of co-operation', and the will to redress all 'natural inequalities'. Here, however, the theory becomes paradoxical. 'One of the effects of a high state of civilization upon character' was a concentration on 'the narrow sphere of the individual's money-getting pursuits'. This assisted growing opulence but undermined much else that Mill valued, especially public virtue. Humanity paid a high price for civilization in 'the relaxation of individual energy and courage; the loss of proud and self-relying independence; the slavery of so large a portion of mankind to artificial wants; their effeminate shrinking from even the shadow of pain; the dull unexciting monotony of their lives, and the passionless insipidity, and absence of any marked individuality, in their characters'. These produced 'the demoralizing effect of great inequalities in wealth and social rank; and the sufferings of the great mass of the people of civilized countries, whose wants are scarcely better provided for than those of the savage'.

Mill eventually settled on what he thought the destination of progress should be. 'Ethology' aimed to demonstrate how some superior societies could serve as models. In 1844, Mill insisted 'that the Norwegian, & German, & French state of society are much better for the happiness of all concerned than the struggling, go-ahead English & American state'. Why? Such societies valued much else besides money; they recognized that treating 'human beings as good machines & therefore as mere machines' was inadequate. 'What does seem to me essential', he wrote elsewhere, 'is that society at large should not be overworked, nor over-anxious about the means of subsistence'. This gives us a sense of what Mill thought the fully developed personality would

look like. There is no doubt that Mill eventually thought that intellectual independence, and the ability to make moral choices which favoured virtue, were ideals which could be attained by all. For the majority this meant eventually superseding both superstition and deference: 'Until they [the people] are well fed, they cannot be well instructed: and until they are well instructed, they cannot emancipate themselves from the double yoke of priestcraft and of reverence for superiors.'

The means of reaching this destination was open debate about everything. Progress involved replacing myths, superstitions, and falsehoods with truth, first among the educated and then the rest. The 'Saint of Rationalism', as Gladstone called him, Mill wrote in 1854 that 'In government, perfect freedom of discussion in all its modes—speaking, writing, and printing—in law and in fact is the first requisite of good because the first condition of popular intelligence and mental progress. All else is secondary.' He reiterated in 1865 that he believed that 'the history of opinions, and of the speculative faculty, has always been the leading element in the history of mankind'. This is one reason why *On Liberty* remains so important to us. In it were present the four main themes which unite Mill's thought: the progress of opinion by open debate; the passage into and through a transitional age; the defence of individuality as a means of proving free will and avoiding cultural and political mediocrity; and the final appeal to utilitarianism as the abiding philosophy of modern life.

* * * *

We return to Mill today, then, chiefly for his accounts of liberty, utilitarianism, and feminism. We argue constantly about freedom of speech, privacy, surveillance, toleration, and encroachments by state authority. We cite Mill in asking whether we have a 'right to offend' or to 'blaspheme', or when principles collide, or value pluralism is urged. We are in a sense all utilitarians today; the increasing popularity of rankings like the World Happiness Index

indicates that gross domestic product and gross national product are poor measures of 'progress' compared to aggregate well-being. Many other Millite themes remain of interest. Mill warns us of the civic weakness and private selfishness of a rights-centred culture where the language of duty is depleted. He reminds us that trust, honesty, transparency, and dedication to the common good should define public service, not corrupt self-aggrandizement. In an age of resurgent nationalism, we recall that Mill found petty nationalism contemptible. As the natural world around us collapses, the appeal of the stationary state and a stable population are obvious. And women have far from the control over their lives that Mill anticipated or wanted. But we might agree with Mill's thought that 'All the grand sources, in short, of human suffering are in a great degree, many of them almost entirely, conquerable by human care and effort.'

Nonetheless, the road towards Mill's utopia remains obscure. Rationalism was central to his agenda: social progress rested on truth-telling, and on constantly clarifying our beliefs. But in a social-media-dominated age we are less likely to see public opinion progressing towards increasing enlightenment. As Mill feared, people often let their feelings dictate their opinions, not the critical scrutiny of ideas. They want 'truths' which make them feel good rather than uncomfortable. Misinformation, disinformation, and downright lying have become much more common in public life than even a few years ago. Distinguishing propaganda from fact is increasingly difficult. Plutocracy makes a mockery of the 'free press'. There are many monopolies, much dumbing down, and much deceit in the 'marketplace of ideas'. Entrenched opinions, especially where religion is concerned, are slow to alter. Claims of the disinterestedness of intellectual elites, when academia is riven with careerism, egotism, and greed, meet with our scepticism. Ideas of a 'clerisy' offend our sense of equality. Progress towards greater equality is surprisingly slow; in the United Kingdom 30 per cent of the land is still owned by the

aristocracy, while bishops still sit in an unelected House of Lords. And 13 countries still decree the death penalty for blasphemy.

Yet in other areas we have advanced well beyond what Mill expected. We have much less confidence today in the moral superiority of 'civilized' over 'barbaric' peoples. Mill did not recognize claims that peoples have a right to govern themselves badly rather than being dominated by others. We do, usually. After Auschwitz, and other genocides, the moral high ground of 'civility' has been largely abandoned. Today we are more inclined to think with Gandhi, when asked what he thought of British civilization, and responded that it would be a good idea. Far from mid-Victorian complacency, we are plagued with well-justified self-doubt among a collision of contending principles and a blizzard of conflicting supposed rights. Value pluralism is the flavour of our times, and Mill, his pleas for experimentalism notwithstanding, sometimes seems to hint at a value monism which is now often challenged; we are still far from the unity of opinion he thought would result from the progress of civilization. Mill would gaze with dismay as even the much-vaunted consensus on the superiority of representative institutions to dictatorships seems to be slipping away in the face of a plethora of 21st-century crises. Populism seems to invoke his worst fears of ignorant majorities. Mill may not provide answers to all our questions. But he had the courage to see what might lie beyond the horizon. His is a rich and provocative legacy to ponder on.

Further reading

The starting-point for all research on Mill is *The Collected Works of John Stuart Mill* (33 vols, Routledge and Kegan Paul and University of Toronto Press, 1963–91). All references here are to this edition.

Background

Burrow, J. W. *Evolution and Society* (Cambridge University Press, 1966).

Burrow, J. W. *Whigs and Liberals: Continuity and Change in English Political Thought* (Clarendon Press, 1988).

Bush, M. L. *What Is Love? Richard Carlile's Philosophy of Love* (Verso, 1998).

Collini, Stefan. *Public Moralists: Political Thought and Intellectual Life in Britain, 1850–1930* (Oxford University Press, 1991).

Dicey, A. V. *Lectures on the Relation between Law and Public Opinion in England during the Nineteenth Century* (Macmillan & Co., 1905).

Fox, Caroline. *Memoirs of Old Friends* (2 vols, Smith, Elder & Co., 1882).

Grote, Mrs. *The Personal Life of George Grote* (John Murray, 1873).

Halévy, Elie. *The Growth of Philosophic Radicalism* (Faber & Gwyer, 1928).

Knights, Ben. *The Idea of the Clerisy in the Nineteenth Century* (Cambridge University Press, 1978).

Morley, John. *Critical Miscellanies* (2nd series, Chapman & Hall, 1877).

Morley, John. *Recollections* (2 vols, Macmillan & Co., 1917).

Russell, Bertrand and Patricia Russell, eds. *The Amberley Papers: Bertrand Russell's Family Background* (2 vols, George Allen & Unwin, 1937).

Solly, Henry. *'These Eighty Years' or, The Story of an Unfinished Life* (Simpkin, Marshall & Co., 1893).

Winch, Donald. *Wealth and Life: Essays on the Intellectual History of Political Economy in Britain, 1848–1914* (Cambridge University Press, 2003).

Biography

Bain, Alexander. *John Stuart Mill: A Criticism. With Personal Recollections* (Longmans, Green & Co., 1882).

Capaldi, Nicholas. *John Stuart Mill: A Biography* (Cambridge University Press, 2004).

Hayek, F. A. *John Stuart Mill and Harriet Taylor* (Routledge & Kegan Paul, 1951).

Jacobs, Jo Ellen. *The Voice of Harriet Taylor Mill* (Indiana University Press, 2002).

Mill, John Stuart and Auguste Comte. *The Correspondence of John Stuart Mill and Auguste Comte*, transl. Oscar A. Haac (Transaction Publishers, 1995).

Packe, Michael St John. *The Life of John Stuart Mill* (Macmillan, 1954).

Reeves, Richard. *John Stuart Mill. Victorian Firebrand* (Atlantic Books, 2007).

General studies

Baum, Bruce. *Rereading Power and Freedom in J. S. Mill* (University of Toronto Press, 2000).

Berger, Fred R. *Happiness, Justice, and Freedom: The Moral and Political Philosophy of John Stuart Mill* (University of California Press, 1984).

Britton, Karl. *John Stuart Mill* (Penguin Books, 1953).

Donner, Wendy. *The Liberal Self: John Stuart Mill's Moral and Political Philosophy* (Cornell University Press, 1991).

Halliday, R. J. *John Stuart Mill* (George Allen & Unwin, 1976).

Hamburger, Joseph. *Intellectuals in Politics: John Stuart Mill and the Philosophic Radicals* (Yale University Press, 1965).

Holthoon, F. L. van. *The Road to Utopia: A Study of John Stuart Mill's Social Thought* (Van Gorcum & Co., 1971).

Kinzer, Bruce. *J. S. Mill Revisited* (Palgrave, 2007).

Laine, Michael, ed. *A Cultivated Mind: Essays Presented to John M. Robson* (University of Toronto Press, 1991).

Levin, Michael. *Mill on Civilization and Barbarism* (Routledge, 2004).

Miller, Dale E. *John Stuart Mill: Moral, Social and Political Thought* (Polity, 2010).

Mueller, Iris Wessel. *John Stuart Mill and French Thought* (University of Illinois Press, 1956).

Pankhurst, Richard. *The Saint-Simonians, Mill and Carlyle* (Sidgwick and Jackson, 1957).

Persky, Joseph. *The Political Economy of Progress: John Stuart Mill and Modern Radicalism* (Oxford University Press, 2016).

Robson, John M. *The Improvement of Mankind: The Social and Political Thought of John Stuart Mill* (University of Toronto Press, 1968).

Rosen, Frederick. *Mill* (Oxford University Press, 2013).

Ryan, Alan. *J. S. Mill* (Routledge and Kegan Paul, 1974).

Ryan, Alan. *The Philosophy of John Stuart Mill* (2nd edn, Macmillan, 1987).

Semmel, Bernard. *John Stuart Mill and the Pursuit of Virtue* (Yale University Press, 1984).

Skorupski, John. *John Stuart Mill* (Routledge & Kegan Paul, 1989).

Skorupski, John. *Why Read Mill Today?* (Routledge, 2006).

Smith, G. W., ed. *John Stuart Mill's Social and Political Thought* (4 vols, Routledge, 1998).

Turk, Christopher. *Coleridge and Mill* (Avebury, 1988).

Wood, John Cunningham, ed. *John Stuart Mill: Critical Assessments* (4 vols, Croom Helm, 1987).

Liberty

Berlin, Isaiah. *Four Essays on Liberty* (Oxford University Press, 1969).

Brink, David O. *Mill's Progressive Principles* (Clarendon Press, 2013).

Claeys, Gregory. 'Mill and Marx on Inequality', in Sven Ove Hansson, ed., 'Special Issue on John Stuart Mill', *Nineteenth-Century Prose*, 47, no. 1 (Spring 2020), pp. 235–58.

Claeys, Gregory. 'Mill, Moral Suasion, and Coercion', in Thom Brooks, ed., *Ethical Citizenship: British Idealism and the Politics of Recognition* (Palgrave-Macmillan, 2014), pp. 79–104.

Claeys, Gregory. *Mill and Paternalism* (Cambridge University Press, 2013).

Cowling, Maurice. *Mill and Liberalism* (Cambridge University Press, 1963).

Frankfurt, Harry G. *The Importance of What We Care About* (Cambridge University Press, 1988).

Gray, John. *Mill on Liberty* (Routledge & Kegan Paul, 1983).

Hamburger, Joseph. *John Stuart Mill on Liberty and Control* (Princeton University Press, 1999).

Himmelfarb, Gertrude. *On Liberty and Liberalism* (Alfred A. Knopf, 1974).

Liberty: Contemporary Responses to John Stuart Mill (Thoemmes Press, 1994).

Riley, Jonathan. *Mill on Liberty* (Routledge, 1998).

Ryan, Alan. *Property and Political Theory* (Basil Blackwell, 1984).

Ten, C. L. *Mill on Liberty* (Clarendon Press, 1980).

Ten, C. L., ed. *Mill's On Liberty: A Critical Guide* (Cambridge University Press, 2008).

Utilitarianism

Cooper, Wesley E., et al., eds. *New Essays on John Stuart Mill and Utilitarianism* (Canadian Association for Publishing in Philosophy, 1979).

Crisp, Roger. *Mill on Utilitarianism* (Routledge, 1997).

Eggleston, Ben, and Dale E. Miller, eds. *The Cambridge Companion to Utilitarianism* (Cambridge University Press, 2014).

Haybron, Daniel M. *Happiness: A Very Short Introduction* (Oxford University Press, 2013).

Layard, Richard. *Happiness: Has Social Science a Clue?* (LSE, 2003).

Lazari-Radek, Katarzyna and Peter Singer. *Utilitarianism: A Very Short Introduction* (Oxford University Press, 2017).

Plamenatz, John. *The English Utilitarians* (Blackwells, 1958).

Ryan, Alan. *J. S. Mill* (Routledge & Kegan Paul, 1974).

Stephen, Leslie. *The English Utilitarians* (3 vols, Duckworth & Co., 1900), vol. 3.

Religion

Crimmins, James. *Secular Utilitarianism: Social Science and the Critique of Religion in the Thought of Jeremy Bentham* (Clarendon Press, 1990).

Robertson, J. M. *Modern Humanists* (Swan Sonnenschein, 1886).

Sell, Alan P. F., ed. *Mill and Religion: Contemporary Responses to Three Essays on Religion* (Thoemmes Press, 1997).

Politics and government

Doyle, Michael W. *The Question of Intervention: John Stuart Mill and the Responsibility to Protect* (Yale University Press, 2015).

Hare, Thomas. *A Treatise on the Election of Representatives* (Longman, Brown, Green, Longmans and Roberts, 1859).

Moir, Martin I., Douglas M. Peers, and Lynn Zastoupil, eds. *J. S. Mill's Encounter with India* (University of Toronto Press, 1999).

Thompson, Dennis. *John Stuart Mill and Representative Government* (Princeton University Press, 1976).

Urbinati, Nadia. *Mill on Democracy* (University of Chicago Press, 2002).

Varouxakis, Georgios. *Liberty Abroad: John Stuart Mill on International Relations* (Cambridge University Press, 2013).

Varouxakis, Georgios. *Mill on Nationality* (Routledge, 2002).

Political economy and empire

Hollander, Samuel. *The Economics of John Stuart Mill* (2 vols, Basil Blackwell, 1985).

Kinzer, Bruce. *England's Disgrace? J. S. Mill and the Irish Question* (University of Toronto Press, 2001).

Lipkes, Jeff. *Politics, Religion and Classical Political Economy in Britain: John Stuart Mill and His Followers* (Macmillan, 1999).

Schwartz, Pedro. *The New Political Economy of J. S. Mill* (Weidenfeld & Nicolson, 1968).

Stokes, Eric. *The English Utilitarians and India* (Clarendon Press, 1959).

Zastoupil, Lynn. *John Stuart Mill and India* (Stanford University Press, 1994).

Feminism

Jacobs, Jo Ellen. *The Voice of Harriet Taylor Mill* (Indiana University Press, 2002).

Morales, Maria H. *Perfect Equality: John Stuart Mill on Well-Constituted Communities* (Rowman and Littlefield, 1996).

Tulloch, Gail. *Mill and Sexual Equality* (Harvester-Wheatsheaf, 1989).

John Stuart Mill

Index

Index

LEADERSHIP
A Very Short Introduction
Keith Grint

In this *Very Short Introduction* Keith Grint prompts the reader to rethink their understanding of what leadership is. He examines the way leadership has evolved from its earliest manifestations in ancient societies, highlighting the beginnings of leadership writings through Plato, Sun Tzu, Machiavelli and others, to consider the role of the social, economic, and political context undermining particular modes of leadership. Exploring the idea that leaders cannot exist without followers, and recognising that we all have diverse experiences and assumptions of leadership, Grint looks at the practice of management, its history, future, and influence on all aspects of society.

www.oup.com/vsi

VERY SHORT INTRODUCTIONS are for anyone wanting a stimulating and accessible way into a new subject. They are written by experts, and have been translated into more than 45 different languages.

The series began in 1995, and now covers a wide variety of topics in every discipline. The VSI library currently contains over 700 volumes—a Very Short Introduction to everything from Psychology and Philosophy of Science to American History and Relativity—and continues to grow in every subject area.

Very Short Introductions available now:

John Stuart Mill: A Very Short Introduction